C000194114

# ONLY IN
# YORKSHIRE

Welcome ter
YORKSHER
Twinned wi' Paradise
QUEEN'S
ENGLISH
NOT
SPOKKEN
'ERE
PHRASE
BOOKS
F' SALE
HOW T'
SPEAK
YORKSHER

# ONLY IN YORKSHIRE

A meandering miscellany of
facts, figures, folklore and legends
that can be found … only in Yorkshire

by Phil Penfold

Dalesman

First published in 2011 by Dalesman
*an imprint of*
Country Publications Ltd
The Water Mill, Broughton Hall
Skipton, North Yorkshire BD23 3AG
www.dalesman.co.uk



ISBN 978-1-85568-295-5



Printed in China by Latitude Press Ltd.

# Author's Introduction

Some of the greatest enjoyment from writing a book, or a feature article or a good news story, is the researching of it. The digging out of the **facts and the wheres and whyfores**, and getting all the details, and that is certainly true of ***Only in Yorkshire***. Any writer who tells you that "research is dull" just isn't researching the right subject!

The funny thing is that **one thing seems to lead to another** … when you get the flavour of one little yarn, another seems to spring up, as a sort of tangent, and you're off and away checking out another story.

I have to admit that when the idea of ***Only in Yorkshire*** was first mooted, I did think that the material would be plentiful, but I was completely astounded at the **sheer amount and the variety of it** that I could delve in to, and (trust me, I'm a journalist) what you will discover in the following pages is just the tip of a very large iceberg. There is an overwhelming amount that we've had to omit. There's plenty more for ***Only in II – The Sequel*** and even ***Only in III – The Saga Continues***, if you'd like to read them.

The Dalesman team and I actively encourage you to get in contact with any ideas or Yorkshire stories that you may have, and we all hope that you'll discover a few **facts, figures and human foibles** within these pages that will jog some memories, amuse, entertain and maybe even elucidate.

**And here's a thought:** Only in Yorkshire would you have the chutzpah, the sheer nerve, to publish a book called ***Only in Yorkshire***, and be very proud of it … 'Only in Rutland', we feel, wouldn't even be a book. It would be a slim pamphlet.

Enjoy!

**Phil Penfold**

*Dedication: for my mother, Neil, Rich, Mark, Judi and Gerry, Tina and Sandy, Jessica and Keith, Bruce and Lyle – all of whom offered more ideas and encouragement than you could possibly imagine…*

**Yorkshire Pudding** is made from a batter and is usually served with a roast beef or pork or lamb, and a rich gravy. Cooks in Yorkshire devised a method of making wheat flour and eggs into a light pudding, using the fat that dripped from the roasting meat. One of the first mentions of the dish **"A dripping pudding"** was in ***The Whole Duty of a Woman,*** published in 1737. But that recipe used mutton, and not beef. A decade later, **Hannah Glasse** came up with a very similar recipe in her ***The Art of Cookery Made Plain and Easy***.

**In 2008 the Royal Society of Chemistry (no less) ruled that:**

***"A Yorkshire Pudding isn't a Yorkshire Pudding if it is less than four inches tall".***

Early versions were much flatter than the familiar puddings of today. Yorkshire Puddings were often offered before the main course of the meat, instead of with it, to take the edge off an appetite and to fill up the eater, who wouldn't then want too much of the following vegetables and meat. Yorkshire Puddings are, after all, a lot less expensive than the rest of the meal's constituents, and made kitchen budgets stretch that little bit further.

A 'scuffler' is something completely different, and in the Yorkshire dialect is a fluffy white bread roll or cake, baked in a roughly triangular form.

**Dock Pudding** is now made chiefly in the Calder Valley area, and particularly in **Mytholmroyd**, using the leaves of the bistort, or ***'gentle dock'*** in addition to young nettles, oatmeal, onions and seasoning to taste. Traditionally it is fried in a pan, with local bacon as an accompaniment.

KEEP OUT
KEEP OUT
KEEP OUT
KEEP OUT
KEEP OUT
YORKSHIRE PUDDING INSPECTION IN PROGRESS
PETE

The traditional folk song ***Scarborough Fair*** was a huge hit for **Simon and Garfunkel** back in 1966, when it featured on their album ***Parsley, Sage, Rosemary and Thyme***, and again in 1968 when it was released as a single after the international success of ***The Graduate***, where it was used as part of the soundtrack.

But why do those particular herbs get a mention in the song?

**It's something that has mystified scholars and singers alike, and has thrown up a whole set of theories.**

**One is that they make up a Pagan love charm...**

...and another is that they were used to ward off the evil of the Plague, or Black Death, and to hide the noxious whiff of death and decay.

The lyrics to the song are all about a lover who tells his listener to ask his former partner to undertake a whole list of impossible tasks (like making a shirt without a seam, and cleaning it in a dry well) so that he can take her back.

Other singers who have recorded the song include Yorkshire's own **Lesley Garrett**, **Marianne Faithful**, **Sarah Brightman**, **Martin Carthy**, **Bryn Terfel**, **Hayley Westenra**, **Nana Mouskouri** and **Harry Belafonte**. That road to Scarborough Fair truly has been well-travelled.

Food Glorious Food

*There are many, many fine Yorkshire cheeses –*

***Wensleydale, Swaledale, Coverdale, Ribblesdale, Ryedale among them,***

and in a bewildering and tasty range of blues, creams and crumblies.

***There's** lavender cheese, pickled onion cheese, chives cheese, **just about every succulent combination that you can think of cheese.***

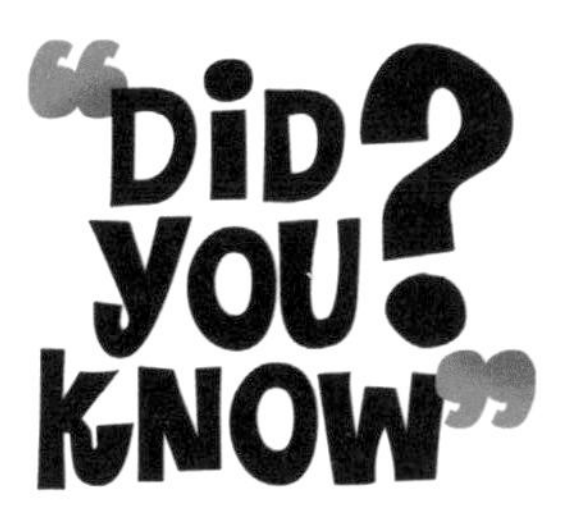


***There are more varieties of cheese made in Yorkshire than anywhere else in Britain today.***

***But beware the EU pen-pushers*** – for today's sheep's milk **Fine Fettle Cheese** had to change its name back in 2007, when a European Union Directive decreed that Feta Cheese could only come from Greece – until then, **Fine Fettle had been called Yorkshire Feta**. Judy Bell, the owner of the makers, **Shepherd's Purse Cheeses**, immediately complied.

RHUBARB
GROWING
SHED
QUIET
PLEASE

**The Rhubarb Triangle** is a nine-square-mile area between **Wakefield**, **Morley** and **Rothwell** – once it was much bigger and stretched out toward **Leeds**, **Bradford** and **Wakefield**. We may not have been able (to date) to persuade the men with the rule books in Brussels that Yorkshire Puddings should be given Protected Designation of Origin status, but our rhubarb got that honour in February 2010, alongside such other top-flight food and drink products like Parma Ham and Champagne.

The cultivation of ***'forced'*** **rhubarb started about 200 years ago,** with fields being fertilised with a rich mixture of animal dung, ***'night soil'*** from nearby towns, and woollen waste from the mungo and shoddy mills.

The plants spend two to three years out in the open and are left unharvested. In November, when the frosts begin, they are taken into unlit but heated sheds (originally the boilers were coal-fired) and the forcing process begins.

**When ready for harvest, the leaves are a sickly yellowy-beige, but the two-foot-long stalks are a rich ruddy crimson – and delicious. In its time outdoors the crown of the plant has absorbed enough energy to transfer the goodness into the stalk when it goes inside. By the end of March, the process is over, and the old root-stock is lifted and used for compost – there is very little waste indeed.**

Traditionally, **indoor rhubarb** is harvested in the softly romantic glow of candlelight – harsh electric light will be detrimental to the product. Many of the farming families growing the rhubarb have been in the trade for generations, and are fiercely proud of the process. One of the farmers, **Janet Oldroyd-Hume** (who has been affectionately dubbed ***'The Rhubarb Queen',*** grows 1,000 tonnes of rhubarb every year, 200 of which is by the forced method. Her family have won medals for their rhubarb, and she claims that if you stand quietly in the sheds –

**Once, Yorkshire grew over ninety per cent of the world's forced rhubarb, but now a lot of it comes from Holland and the Low Countries.**
**Beware of imitations!**

***"you can hear the rhubarb grow".***

Janet believes that the revival in the love for rhubarb lies in the current enjoyment of tartness in our food, and the fact that it is rich in potassium and calcium, both of which are thought to help in lowering cholesterol, and in preventing deep vein thrombosis.

Where does the name come from? The Roman name for the River Volga was *Rha*. The Rha was a boundary between the civilised world and the Barbarians, or *Barbarum*. The plant grew plentifully on the river banks. Put all that together, and...

Rhubarb is a native of Siberia, which is probably why it seems to enjoy the cold wet winters of this part of Yorkshire

But it suffers from an identity crisis – some cookbooks refer to it as a vegetable, others put it in the fruit category.

The first **Bettys** (note the lack of apostrophe) tea room was opened in Harrogate, on Cambridge Crescent, in 1919, just after the end of the First World War. It later moved to its present location, in Parliament Street.

The Bettys chain now has (to date) six cafés, each with a shop. They can be found in Harrogate – the Parliament Street branch and another at RHS Harlow Carr – two in York, in Ilkley and Northallerton.

## YORKSHIRE GREATS

*The branch of Bettys in* **St Helen's Square in York** *was a favourite haunt of Canadian and US servicemen during the war – thousands of them were stationed as* **'Bomber boys'** *around the city, and many signed their names on a mirror in the café, using a diamond pen.*

**Henderson's Relish** is the infinitely superior Yorkshire version of Worcestershire sauce, *and contains no anchovies* which makes it the favourite of the two for vegetarians.

Made in Sheffield for over a century, it has found favour with folk as famous as **Sean Bean**, **David Blunkett MP**, **Richard Hawley** and **Peter Stringfellow** as well as countless ***'rank and file'*** customers.

***A special mix of spices is combined with a closely-guarded secret recipe, and every once in a while a rumour goes around that the owner of Henderson's is about to retire, and that he will take the recipe with him. This is never ever true.***

Henderson's has been the subject of poems, songs and even artworks, and no local dish has ever quite achieved the loyalty that Henderson fans give unswervingly to the product.

RELISH
RECIPE
'ANDS OFF
RELISH

BLESSED ARE THOSE WHO
DO NOT ASK FOR TICK
SWEAR YE NOT!
NO
IFFY
JOKES

There was an unlikely buyer for the **Fox and Hounds Inn** at **Carlton in Cleveland** when it came up for sale just over a century ago. It was a profitable business, because the village (about three miles south of Stokesley) was a jolly jaunt away from the conurbation of Teesside, and at the weekends visitors would flock to the picturesque spot to have a stroll and then a drink. And maybe another drink as well. In fact, it became a place associated with a good Sunday brawl. **So who was the new owner?**

Step forward **the village vicar, Canon J L Kyle,** who immediately applied for a change to a six-day licence, so that intoxicating liquor could not be sold on the Holy Day, and who added tea and light refreshments to the inn's facilities.

**Canon Kyle was nothing if not versatile. When he wasn't in the pulpit, out fund-raising or behind the saloon bar pulling pints, he was also something of a farmer, and had a flock of prize-winning black-faced sheep.**

Canon Kyle was not a man to be trifled with. He was appointed to the living when the village had no church – it had been burned down in 1881 in circumstances which had never been fully explained. The Rev Kyle immediately set to, raised funds for a new building (which still stands) and later added the tower plus a peal of bells.

A strange encounter took place (so entertainment legend has it) on the stage of the **Batley Variety Club** sometime in the early 1980s.

**Mike and Bernie Winters** had been a phenomenally successful double act for many years. The brothers toured all over the UK, and had appeared many, many times on television.

**But, like many double acts before them, they fell out, and the act was dissolved in 1978, because the animosity between them had grown too much. Mike emigrated to the USA, and Bernie, alongside a huge St Bernard dog called Schnorbitz, went on performing, and hosted several popular TV game shows.**

Bernie was in cabaret at the famous Batley venue one night, and sadly he wasn't going down too well with his audience. And Mike had, by chance, made a visit to the UK. Mike clearly felt that the timing was right for a reconciliation and, unknown to Bernie, went to Batley to see his estranged sibling. Watching the show, he saw clearly that things were not going as they should be – Bernie wasn't getting the laughs. So he went out of the club, round to the stage door, in, and onto the stage with a hand outstretched, and ready to shake…

…there was a stunned silence from the paying punters until one of them spoke. "Blimey," he said incredulously, **"There's ruddy TWO on 'em!"**

The renowned conductor **Sir Thomas Beecham** was relaxing with a cigar and a brandy after a symphony concert in the late thirties. Across the lobby of (it is said) the **Queen's Hotel** in **Leeds,** he saw a woman who he knew well, but he was having trouble remembering her name.

As she passed, he stood up, and doffed his Homburg hat. The memory sparked into life – he knew her brother!

***"Good evening Sir Thomas," said the mystery lady. "That was a wonderful concert tonight, the Delius was very moving."***

*"Thank you so much," said the Baronet, "that is most kind of you. And, er, how is your brother?"*

***"Ah," said the lady graciously. "He's very well, and he's still king."***

Sir Thomas had greeted **Princess Mary,** The Princess Royal, and the Countess of Harewood, sister to George VI and daughter to George V.

Despite all the alleged jollity and camaraderie of showbusiness, things have not always been sweetness and light between performers.

In 1869, one of the greatest stars of the day, **George Leybourne** (celebrated for his songs ***Champagne Charlie*** and ***The Man on the Flying Trapeze***, among many others), was appearing at **Sheffield's Alexandra Opera House and Music Hall**, and staying at the city's **Victoria Hotel**.

On a Friday evening in early March, and after his show, he was in the lobby of the hotel when another artiste, **Tom Fancourt** (who was on the bill at the rival Royal Pavilion Music Hall), approached him and accused him of trying to ruin his, Fancourt's, professional reputation in the town.

According to Fancourt, Leybourne didn't say anything, but hit him with a stroke that knocked his hat over his eyes, and then there was another blow to the ear. **Mr Brelsford,** the clearly diplomatic owner of the Victoria, said later that he had seen ***"some wrangling"*** between the two parties, but hadn't observed that punches were exchanged.

**Unfortunately, reports Christopher Beeching (a former long-time Hebden Bridge resident) in his meticulously researched biography on Leybourne, *The Heaviest of Swells*, the whole silly business came to court, where Leybourne was found guilty and fined a shilling (five pence) with eight shillings (forty pence) costs.**

He then paid £2 into court, and asked that the excess of the fine went into the local poor box. Fancourt's solicitor was heard to say, ***"Oh that's only an advertisement"***. It certainly didn't do Leybourne any harm – he went on in the following weeks to fill halls and theatres in Leeds and Bradford.

***Yorkshire can lay claim to two (and possibly three) of the world's most prolific playwrights.***

The first is **Sir Alan Ayckbourn**, who to many is simply ***'Mr Scarborough'***, since he has had a long and fruitful association with the town's **Stephen Joseph Theatre** since 1957. He has said that, back then, he hadn't got a clue where Scarborough was, and when he was told that there might be a job as stage manager and actor for him up there (he was born in Hampstead in London) he had to ask for directions.

**"They told me 'Go up to York on the train, get off, and turn right.' Which is what I did."**

And the second is his colleague, just down the coast, **John Godber**. Godber is equally ***'Mr Hull'***. Godber was born in **Upton**, near Pontefract, and until the very early months of 2011 was associated with **Hull Truck Theatre**. There was a parting of the ways, and Godber (and his wife, the actress **Jane Thornton**) are now banging the drum for drama at Wakefield's beautiful **Theatre Royal and Opera House**, one of the surviving theatrical gems designed by the genius that was **Frank Matcham**.

**Both men have had triumphs on their home turf, throughout the UK and the world, and in the West End of London.**

Sir Alan has received more than thirty-five awards (to time of writing) including a pair of Olivier's, a Tony, a Molière and three Lifetime Achievement Awards, one from the Variety Club of Great Britain, one from the Critics' Circle, and another from The Writers' Guild. He was knighted for his considerable services to the theatre in 1997. He officially stepped down from the post of Artistic Director of the SJT in 2009, but his output continues, for in 2011 he wrote an adaptation of *Uncle Vanya*, called *Dear Uncle*, and a completely new play called *Neighbourhood Watch*.

He has said that he always has a new play somewhere in the back of his mind, to start when the last one is finished and presented. To date, he has written seventy-four full-length plays, but by the time that this book is on the shelves, that could be seventy-five. Or seventy-six! Among them are ***The Norman Conquests***, ***Bedroom Farce***, ***Haunting Julia*** and ***House and Garden***.

YORKSHIRE GREATS

In comparison, Mr Godber is a mere beginner, with only (only!) fifty-two plays under his belt. They include ***Bouncers***, ***Teechers***, ***Up 'n' Under***, ***Lucky Sods*** and ***Men of the World***. Like Ayckbourn, he is an observer of life and the foibles of ordinary folk – particularly Yorkshiremen – and one of his plays, ***Wrestling Mad***, was based on a bout that he once saw in Bridlington. He was made Professor of Contemporary Drama at Liverpool Hope University in 2004, and has been visiting Professor of Drama at Hull University for three years.

And the third great dramatist? How about **Ernest Wiseman**, born in East

Ardsley, between Wakefield and Leeds, in November 1925. **Ernest Wiseman** was the son of Harry, a railway porter, and there were another six brothers and sisters. Money was short, and his mother Connie fought a constant battle with the cashflow. Harry and his father before him were singers on the northern working men's clubs circuit, and it was no surprise when little Ernest showed that he had a theatrical streak in him. The lad became a tap dancer, and he and his father then toured a double act as **Bert Carson and His Little Wonder**.

GUESS WHO

**Ernest hated school, and looked out for any opportunity to put it behind him. In 1936 he joined a show for youngsters, The Nignog Revue, at the Bradford Alhambra, and appeared with it on several occasions.**

An impresario called **Bryan Mitchie** (think of Hughie Green and *Opportunity Knocks*) was touring the north looking for new talent, and he spotted Ernest on stage. Ernest auditioned, and thought that he'd done quite well, but heard nothing for months.

**But Mitchie had mentioned the lad to Jack Hylton, the Simon Cowell of his day, and Ernest was summoned to London and auditioned again, in Hylton's offices above the Prince's (now the Shaftesbury) Theatre.**

PLAYS WOT
I WROTE
by
Ernie Wise

Hylton was so impressed that he put him into a show that evening, and made the lad sign a three-year contract. He also asked him if he'd change his name. Ernest said he wouldn't mind.

*He went into Hylton's offices as Ernest Wiseman, and emerged as Ernie Wise.*

And **Ernie Wise**, as we all know, gave us dozens of television's most memorable dramas in the ***Plays Wot I Wrote***, which were part of the immensely popular **Morecambe and Wise** shows for both ITV and the BBC. Ernie died in 1999, aged seventy three and still working in a solo career after Eric's death a few years before.

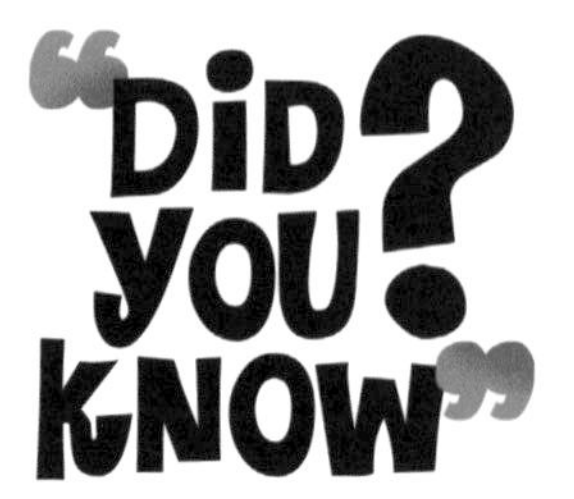


Who else but Ernie and Eric could persuade the likes of **Glenda Jackson, Sir Alec Guinness, Laurence Olivier, John Thaw, Andre Previn** and **Peter Cushing** (to name only a few) to appear in their excruciatingly bad but hilariously funny plays?

There is now a seven-foot-high statue to Ernie in Morley – he used to perform in the town's Pavilion Theatre. It cost £8,000, and was sculpted by local artist Melanie Wilks.

**The Georgian Theatre** in **Richmond, North Yorkshire**, first opened its doors in 1788. It was built by the Andrew Lloyd-Webber of his day, a **Mr Samuel Butler**, a theatrical impresario who had a chain of theatres throughout the county in Whitby, Beverley, Harrogate, Ripon and Northallerton, and another pair 'over the border' in Ulverston and Kendal.

Richmond's Georgian Theatre is Grade I listed, and there is evidence that when the first audiences entered the auditorium all those years ago, they were mightily impressed by the scenery, which was painted by local Royal Academician George Cuit the Elder.

The theatre is Britain's most complete playhouse of its kind and period, and it thrives to this day.

Today's re-created front drop-cloth is a reproduction of one of Cuit's paintings of Richmond Castle above the River Swale, which he created in 1810.

The Georgian Theatre is internationally known as a living museum of the theatre community, but it also plays a much-loved and highly significant role in Richmond itself, and is highly valued by local people.

**It is probably a little fanciful to equate Holmfirth with Hollywood, but the little town made famous by the BBC's long-running *Last of the Summer Wine* was actually, for a very short period before the First World War, something of a major production base for films.**

The passion for film followed other Victorian crazes – and not long after the **Lumière brothers** in France started to produce their films, Yorkshire firms such as **Riley Brothers** of **Bradford** were making motion picture cameras. Don't forget that in the late 1880s **Louis Aimé Augustin Le Prince,** one of the great film pioneers, had filmed two scenes in **Leeds** at **Roundhay Garden** and **Leeds Bridge**, and is considered by many film historians to be the real and only father of film as we know it today.

Mysteriously, Le Prince vanished on a trip to France only two years later, and was never able to get what his heart desired – a patent for his invention in the US.

**Was Le Prince murdered, or did he commit suicide? Was his death just a tragic accident?**

The only clue is that, a century after his disappearance and (presumed) death, French police found a photograph in an old archive of a man who looked like Louis.

Louis' films were never shown to a commercial audience, but they were demonstrated in the factory owned by his patron **James Whitely**, of Whitely Partners in Hunslet, and in the Whitely home, Oakwood Grange, in Roundhay. Louis also married Whitely's sister, **Elizabeth James**. There is a blue plaque noting his achievements on Leeds Bridge to this day.

HOLMFIRTH

**James Bamforth** of **Holmfirth** also became fascinated by the possibilities of the new medium, and would have been aware of the story of **Le Prince,** and how he was last seen boarding a train in Dijon with his luggage. James was already a widely respected manufacturer of slides for ***'magic lanterns'***, and was a talented artist who painted elaborate backdrops for his subjects. Not only that –

– he was also a persuasive man who could charm his neighbours and townsfolk into appearing in various poses and positions. What could be easier than a transition from static scenes into moving pictures?

He began turning out picture after picture, and the demand for the output grew and grew. He also created one of the first film ***'characters'*** with a comic personality all his own, a chap called **Winky,** whose antics delighted the audiences. He was played by a local called **Reginald Twisk**, who is almost completely forgotten a century later. Another of Bamforth's favoured actors was the Holmfirth blacksmith **Fred Bullock**, who would often get the call to come along and make an appearance. Clearly Bamforth had some charm (and also chutzpah) because the smith would down irons and oblige.

**One of the Holmfirth bank managers was generous enough to allow his building to be used in hold-up and robbery scenes, and Holmfirth station and the local railway also played many a part.**

***Who needed elaborate sets when you were right in the middle of one of the best locations in the country?***

Today, experts believe that Bamforth was among the first to capture comedy (albeit in the slapstick tradition) on film. Sadly, little footage exists today, and the whole enterprise ground rather suddenly to a halt just as it was getting into its stride. How so?

Well, in August 1914 Archduke Franz Ferdinand of Austria, and his morganatic wife, Sophie Duchess of Hohenberg, were shot dead in Sarajevo by Gavrilo Princip, one of six Bosnian Serb conspirators. Their open-topped car had taken a wrong turning, the chauffeur reversed the vehicle slowly, and Princip seized his chance. On such minor matters history turns.

This violent act triggered a collapse like a pile of dominoes, and before a few days were out, all of Europe was mobilising, one country at war with each other.

**Britain's war effort** knew no bounds, and filming stopped as men enlisted, and vital materials were diverted to the cause. Making movies seemed a frivolous occupation, and a lot of old film stock was – unbelievably – rendered down for the metals it contained. **That's why so many early British films have simply vanished.**

Across the other side of the Atlantic, however, America wasn't at war – not for some time – and the film-makers in New York and then in California seized the moment.

Film was, of course, silent, so there was no language barrier at all – it could be seen and appreciated anywhere. **Hollywood** rose to dominance,

SAUCY
POSTCARDS

**Holmfirth** slipped into obscurity – as far as the film industry was concerned.

But **James Bamforth** was not a man to give up in business. He turned his hand to producing postcards (the company is still going strong, although it has left family hands, and is now based in **Leeds**). His first popular series were highly sentimental depictions of Tommy wistfully yearning for his wife (or sweetheart) and family at home. Others had verses from popular songs of the day.

***They were sentimental, kitsch, and sold in their hundreds of thousands.***

After the war, Bamforth changed direction, and his postcards (they are all much sought-after) turned to another British institution – **the seaside**. His saucy (some would say 'lewd') pictures of big-busted viragos, cuckolded husbands, drunken middle-aged men, amorous couples and nubile young women, all with suggestive captions (***"I can't see my little Willie anywhere!"***), sailed very very close to the wind, but captured the British love of vulgarity and double entendre. The ones illustrated by **Donald McGill** were particularly popular and rude – work from a man who had been at school with a future **Bishop of Wakefield!** They often incurred the wrath of the censor, and McGill on one occasion was hauled into court and his wrists firmly slapped.

But, showing a true Yorkshire businessman's approach to matters financial, the Bamforth company never paid McGill more than three guineas (£3.15) for any illustration, even at the height of his fame. There were no royalties, either.

If film history was made in Yorkshire, then so was that of the small screen.

The county can be proud of its close association with four of the longest-running TV series of all time – **All Creatures Great and Small, Heartbeat, Last of the Summer Wine** (which was loved and loathed in about equal measures) and Yorkshire's very own soap, **Emmerdale**.

The first three, in particular, made (and still make) a huge impact on the local economy, persuading visitors in their droves to spend time in Herriot Country ***(around Thirsk and Richmond in North Yorkshire)***, in Heartbeat Country ***(around Goathland)***, and Summer Wine Country, which is the area around ***Holmfirth***.

## YORKSHIRE GREATS

***Summer Wine*** was created by **Austerfield** writer **Roy Clarke**, and began life as a one-off for the ***Comedy Playhouse*** series. That episode was first aired in January 1973, and the eventual series went on from there, only finishing in 2010, when the BBC waved a flag of surrender and pulled the plug.

***In all there were thirty-one series, several specials and two full-length films.***

They all focused on a dysfunctional set of men in their later years, and their relationships with their families and neighbours. The original trio consisted of **Bill Owen** as Compo (Owen was in fact a Londoner, and made an early living in films and TV playing cheerful 'Cockney sparrer' types), **Peter Sallis** as the deep-thinking Clegg (Sallis was in the original London production of ***Cabaret***, with Yorkshire's very own **Judi Dench**, before her damehood, and playing probably the best Sally Bowles anywhere, anytime, nohow), and **Michael Bates** as the snobbish and "do it my way, not yours", Blamire. Bates had to drop out after only two series, due to ill-health.

**When Bill Owen died in 1999, he was replaced by his real-life son Tom Owen, who joined up to play ... Tom. Not a very inventive leap of name, perhaps? Other names associated with the series have been Russ Abbott, Bert Kwouk, Brian Murphy, the splendid Dame Thora Hird, Jean Alexander, Kathy Staff, Jean Ferguson and Dora Bryan, to name but a few.**

With Bates' departure, his shoes were filled over the years by **Brian Wilde** as war veteran Foggy, the bonkers inventor Seymour, played by **Michael Aldridge**, and then the former policeman Truly, played by **Frank Thornton**.

The delight for visitors to **Holmfirth** is that they can readily identify the locations in which the series was filmed – such as **Nora Batty's house** and **Sid's Café**.

And the same could be said of the loyal fans of ***Heartbeat***, the ITV series which was given the axe – completely without warning to cast or crew – after eighteen series in 2010. Like ***Summer Wine***, it was once the firm staple of Sunday night viewing.

Based on the Constable novels by **Nicholas Rhea** (the pen-name of Peter Walker, himself a former copper) ***Heartbeat*** focused on the fictional communities of **Aidensfield** and **Ashfordly**, but most of the filming was done in and around the very real **Goathland**, and quite a lot on the **North Yorkshire Moors Railway**. It was originally written as a vehicle for **Nick Berry**, who had, in 1992, just left ***EastEnders***, the soap, and who was looking for a suitably different vehicle for his talents.

*Heartbeat* was set in the sixties, and revived an interest in the music of the period – Berry even got to Number Two in the charts when he recorded a cover version of the Buddy Holly hit after which the show was named.

He was cast as PC Nick Rowan, a London lad transferred, along with his doctor wife Kate, to the North York Moors. The loveable rogue of the series, until ill-health forced him to quit the show, was played by **Bill Maynard**, and when Maynard left, by **Geoffrey Hughes**.

Yorkshire TV produced all the series, and had another hit with a spin-off series set in a local hospital, ***The Royal***, which starred, among other major names, one of Yorkshire's finest-ever actors, the late and much-missed **Ian Carmichael**.

**When ITV amalgamated all their local stations under one umbrella, Yorkshire TV was, to all intents and purposes, wiped out, and the TV Centre, on Kirkstall Road in Leeds, once a hive of activity, became a rather ghostly, echoing place.**

The axe fell on ***The Royal*** at the same time as it did on ***Heartbeat***, and despite loud protests from fans, there was to be no reprieve.

**All Creatures Great and Small** was based on the books of the Yorkshire vet **Alf Wight**, who wrote under the pen name of **James Herriot**. Set in the early series before the Second World War, it picked up again in the post-war period for later stories.

**Christopher Timothy** played James Herriot, **Robert Hardy** (who was to become inextricably involved with the Royal Armouries in Leeds) was Siegfried Farnon, and **Carol Drinkwater** was Helen Herriot in the first three series, while **Lynda Bellingham** played the role in the last four. *All Creatures* started in 1978, and finished its very respectable run in 1990.

GOD'S OWN COUNTRY

***The outdoor locations for the series included Feetham in Swaledale, Bolton Castle, Askrigg, and Langthwaite in Arkengarthdale. Indoor locations were shot in the delightful surroundings of the BBC's then flagship studios in Birmingham.***

The interior set of the dispensary in **Skeldale House**, the base for Herriot and his colleagues the Farnon brothers, is now on display in the **Herriot Museum** in **Thirsk**.

***Emmerdale*** went on screen a year earlier than ***Summer Wine***, in 1972, and was first known as ***Emmerdale Farm***, and was created by **Kevin Laffan**. The executive producer for nearly a quarter of a century was **Keith Richardson**, who had actually worked on the very first episode, in a rather more lowly capacity. The idea is rather similar to Radio 4's *The Archers*, in that Emmerdale focuses on a farming community, and the characters that live in it.

It is still made in part at the old Yorkshire TV studios, but is chiefly filmed on a specially built full-size location set just outside Leeds, on the **Harewood Estate**.

It has been much enlivened by a cargo plane crashing on the village, by innumerable car smashes, and by explosions a-plenty. Not to mention shootings, murders, rapes, and lightning strikes.

***Emmerdale is NOT the place to live if you want to lead a quiet life.***

The show started outside location work in the village of **Esholt**, but its fast-growing popularity meant that fans turned up in droves, and filming was often interrupted. The only solution was to replicate Emmerdale somewhere quieter. In Esholt, the Commercial Hotel had to have its signage changed every time it was in camera shot – in ***Emmerdale*** the local is called the ***Woolpack***. When the series left for their new home, the then landlord thought it would be simpler just to leave the Woolpack sign where it was, and it remains the Woolpack to this day.

***Summer Wine, All Creatures Great and Small, Heartbeat*** **and *The Royal* may all have ceased production, but they can all still be found, somewhere or other, on the dozens of satellite channels that are now available. In that bizarre TV-land, Compo, Clegg and their mates are forever young, and James Herriot is always just about to put on his rubber gloves for another calving.**

Many performers have claimed to have 'died' on stage, when they have failed to achieve the attention or adulation from the audience that they feel that they deserve. But one much-loved star actually breathed his last on the stage of one of Yorkshire's ***'lost'*** theatres, the **Tivoli** in **Hull**.

**Arthur Lucan**, better known as **Old Mother Riley**, was waiting in the wings in May 1954, fell ill, collapsed and died. His understudy, **Roy Rolland**, didn't hesitate –

***"I was already in an identical costume, so I took the still warm wig from his head, went on, and did the act."***

Whether anyone actually noticed the substitution at the time isn't known. The Tivoli has long since been demolished, but there is a bakery and café on the site today, and in a corner there is a bust to the music hall and British movie legend, with some of his personal memorabilia.

Forget that upstart Dick Turpin. It wasn't he who rode from London to York in a single day, but Pontefract's very own **'Swift Nick Nevison'**. John (or James, or William, make your own choice)

Nevison was born in South Yorkshire in 1639, troubled times indeed. Just into his teens, he ran away from home after stealing from his own father. He made his way to London, had a few adventures and then joined the army of the **Duke of York**, serving with some distinction at the **Siege of Dunkirk**. He returned to England, and took up the lucrative profession of stealing from travellers on the **Great North Road** – in particular the stretch from Nottingham up into Yorkshire. He was supposed to have been a fairly gallant rogue, and one day Nevison hit the headlines.

In 1676, when Charles II was back on the throne, he was working a stretch of what is now the A2, in Kent, when a sailor hove into view. It was early morning. Nevison robbed the man at a place called Gad's Hill (Charles Dickens was to build his home there, centuries later) and, fearing that the matelot had recognised him, took to his horse and fled.

In fact, he took the ferry across the Thames, and kept going. And going. He got to **Chelmsford**, and then to **Cambridge**, and **Huntingdon** ... and he ended up in the centre of York.

A bowls match was going on, and who else but the city's Lord Mayor was

playing. Bold as brass, Nevison asked His Worship if he could join in, and the men actually had a wager on the outcome.

Some short time afterwards, Nevison was arrested and tried for the Gad's Hill robbery, and he called the Lord Mayor as one of his witnesses.

***Who on earth, he asked, could possibly be in Kent in the morning, and 200 miles north by late afternoon? And hadn't the Lord Mayor enjoyed the match?***

**Result**? An acquittal on the Kentish robbery charge – and nickname of ***'Swift Nick'*** bestowed by his **Gracious Majesty, Charles** himself. However, he was found guilty of theft on other charges, and transported to **Tangier**, then a British colony, and sentenced to several years' hard labour.

Back on home turf again, Nick resumed his career on the highways, and did quite well until his luck ran out.

He was napping in the bar of the Three Houses Inn at Sandal Magna near Wakefield when the law burst in and caught him. Some stories say that he had been betrayed for a bounty placed on his head. Nick had murdered a young constable, Darcy Fletcher, who had tried to arrest him after a robbery near Batley. It is the only time that we know of that he had used violence.

Swift Nick came to trial in **York** in 1684, was found guilty, and hanged at York Castle only days later. He was buried in an unmarked spot in **St Mary's** graveyard. And that shameless imposter **Dick Turpin** went on to get all the credit.

Turpin too was hanged in York, at Knavesmire, and years after Nick, so the two could never ever possibly have met. Turpin went to the gallows in 1739, after being 'shopped' by a schoolmaster who recognised his handwriting on a letter that Turpin had sent to his brother, asking for money to stand bail.

"ah'M FaiR caPPeD"

One story has it that Turpin was arrested at the Blue Bell in Beverley (now called the Beverley Arms) and another locates his arrest at the Green Dragon in Welton, about ten miles from Hull.

Whichever you choose, young Dick wasn't exactly being discreet in his behaviour. He'd been rustling horses in Lincolnshire, got the beasts to swim the Humber at the lowest tide, got drunk, and shot at a gamekeeper. Later it emerged that he was already a wanted man – he'd been robbing travellers on Hampstead Heath.

After his death, he was cut down, and, like Nick, was buried in an unmarked grave after being exhibited in the **Blue Boar Inn** in **York**. He lies in **St George's churchyard**.

Both Swift Nick and Dick Turpin were hanged alone, and not on the notorious **Three-Legged Mare**, a device that is peculiar to Yorkshire.

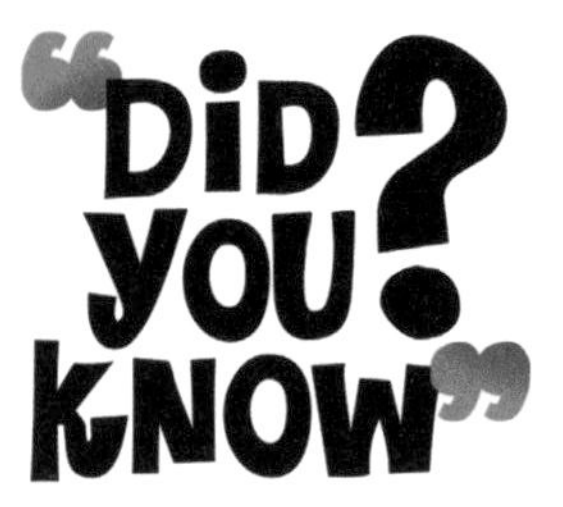


The Mare is a curious but effective device. It consists of three upright posts, several yards high and several feet apart. Across the posts are three stout beams, each with three or four dangling nooses. It was situated at York's Tyburn, not far from the site of today's celebrated racecourse.

The prisoners to be hanged would be trundled up on a low cart, in front of the rowdy crowd. They would each have a noose put around their necks, a prayer would be said, the driver of the cart would flick his whip, the horse would amble off, and the condemned would be left hanging. A sort of executioner's grim conveyor belt, if you like.

The last public hanging in **York** was in 1801. But the Three-Legged Mare device is today commemorated in the name of a very agreeable pub in **High Petergate**. It is affectionately known to its customers as ***'The wonky donkey'***. Think about it.

***Thomas Chippendale**, one of the greatest furniture-makers that the world has ever known, **was born near Otley** (probably in the small community of Farnley) in 1718.*

# YORKSHIRE GREATS

He was the only child of John Chippendale, a joiner, and the young lad got a decent but rudimentary education at **Prince Henry's Grammar School**. When he left there, he did some training with his father – the Chippendales had been making all manner of things with timber for generations – and then went to York to work for the appropriately-named Richard Wood. After that, Thomas headed for London, was twice married, slowly developed his business and published a hugely important book of his designs in 1754 – the very first cabinet-maker to do so.

**His work became an essential part of the grand houses of England – for those who had the money to commission him. In Yorkshire alone, Chippendale's wonderful furniture can be seen in Newby Hall, Temple Newsham, Burton Constable Hall, Nostell Priory and Harewood House.**

He died, respected and admired, in 1779, and a statue to him stands outside his old school in Otley. There is also a huge sculpted representation of Chippendale on the façade of the **Victoria and Albert Museum** in London.

**If someone described you as "pleasant of approach and cheerful of manner, opposed to quarrels and strife", you'd probably be pretty pleased (in your own quiet, modest way) with yourself. That's how one of Guy Fawkes's chums summed him up, and yet poor old Guy has gone down in history as one of the blackest villains of all time, vilified by all, and burned in effigy on countless numbers of bonfires on 5th November.**

**Guy Fawkes** was born in **Stonegate** in **York** in early April, 1570 (the exact date isn't known) and he was christened in the church of **St Michael le Belfrey**, in the shadow of the mighty **Minster**, on 16th April. His father's family were Protestants, but his mother's were secret Catholics. He went to **St Peter's School** in **York**, which also had a great many Catholic links. After his education finished, he went into the service of the first **Viscount Montagu**, who took a dislike to the young man, and fired him. Possibly to spite his grandfather, the second Viscount (who succeeded to the title at the age of eighteen) re-hired Fawkes when the older man shuffled off this mortal coil.

When **James I and VI** succeeded Elizabeth I on the English throne he

**Guy inherited his father's estate at Clifton, and then went off to Europe to fight on the side of the Spanish in their battles with the Dutch. He became more and more politicised, and more and more a fervent Catholic.**

GUNPOWDE
GUNPOWDE
GUNPOWD
GUNPOWDE
GUNPOWDE

started plotting to remove the new king, and to have him replaced. Guy was received at the Spanish court, but wasn't given the active support he needed. Back in England, he joined a group of conspirators led by **Robert Catesby** who planned to assassinate James. They met, as all good conspirators ought to, in a pub, the **Duck and Drake**, in the Strand in **London**.

Guy and his colleagues rented an undercroft room directly beneath the **House of Lords**, and began filling it with gunpowder and firewood. The whole thing was set to go up when the King opened parliament. But **Lord Monteagle** had received an anonymous letter, which told his lordship that it might be wise to stay away from the ceremonies, and Monteagle passed the information on. Monteagle told the king, the king had the cellars searched in the early hours of 5th November, and Guy was arrested leaving the undercroft.

*When questioned, and asked why he was in possession of so much explosive, he replied it was for "blowing you Scottish beggars back to your native mountains."*

After the gentler examinations of the **King's Privy Chamber**, Guy was sent for torture in the Tower of London. He had, up until then, invented a fictitious name for himself – **John Johnson** – and had made up a story about being of a North Yorkshire family.

Under torture, the truth came out, and he signed a confession – he was barely able to scrawl 'Guido Fawkes'. Sent for trial, he and the other conspirators were almost immediately **sentenced to be hung, drawn and quartered.**

On the last day of January, 1606, Guido and another three of the group of plotters were dragged from the Tower on wattle hurdles, and paraded through the streets of London, until they arrived in Old Palace Yard, Westminster.

**He was the last to be killed, and although feeble from constant torture, managed to break free from the hangman, and leaped from the scaffold – breaking his own neck in the process.**

On 5th November 1605, Londoners were encouraged to light bonfires to rejoice in the safety of their King and his ***'joyful deliverance'***, and a tradition had started.

His body was butchered, and various body parts sent out to the corners of the kingdom as a warning to others. There were thirteen men involved in the plot to kill James – only one of them, Guy, is properly remembered to this day.

A famous (or perhaps infamous?) Knaresborough resident of centuries ago was **Eugene Aram**, who was a noted scholar and schoolteacher. As well as a murderer. He was born at **Ramsgill** and became the schoolmaster at **Netherdale**, marrying while still young. Although his background was humble, he taught himself both Latin and Greek. In 1734 he came to **Knaresborough**, and went about his respectable business until 1745, the year of the **Bonnie Prince Charlie** uprising. It was also the year that a man called **Daniel Clark**, a close friend of Aram, persuaded a lot of the merchants to part with a lot of their goods – and disappeared into the night.

Deeply suspicious after being swindled, the merchants began to believe that Aram might be implicated, and his house and garden were searched, and some of the stolen property recovered. But nothing could be effectively pinned on Eugene, and he was able to leave town, and went to London, leaving Mrs Aram at home to pick up the pieces. For years he travelled around England, teaching and writing, and becoming a leading expert on the origin and derivation of words.

*All might have been well had not a skeleton been discovered back at Knaresborough, and a man called Houseman was questioned.*

He said that he'd been present at the murder of Clark by Aram and another man called **Terry**, but then dropped the bombshell that the skeleton wasn't that of Clark at all – and immediately led the investigators to the real spot where Clark's body lay – in **St Robert's Cave**, not far from the town.

Aram was arrested, and brought to York for trial. He pleaded not guilty, and submitted a spirited defence, part of which was that the bones could not be definitively identified – they could be of any old Tom, Dick or Hermit. But poor old Eugene was sent to be hanged, and the noose went around his neck at York's Tyburn in August 1759. While in his cell he had finally admitted that he had killed Clark – after discovering an affair between him and his wife.

The story fascinated many writers in the following years. **Thomas Hood** wrote the ***Ballad of Eugene Aram***, **Bulwer Lytton** wrote a romance about him, **P G Wodehouse** included a reference to him in ***Jeeves Takes Charge***, ***Stiff Upper Lip, Jeeves*** and in ***Summer Lightning***, and **George Orwell** also referenced him in ***A Happy Vicar I Might Have Been***.

Best of all, however, it was the TV psychic and seer **Derek Acorah** who felt the spirit of Aram in his programme ***Most Haunted Live***, in 2004. At the time, he was searching for the shade of **Dick Turpin**.

Surely one of the most multi-talented Yorkshiremen of all time was the late **Brian Glover** (born in **Sheffield** in 1934) who grew up in **Barnsley** and who was not only a hugely versatile actor across a range of genres, from **Shakespeare** (with the **RSC**) to pantomime, but a teacher – of English and French – a writer with over twenty plays and short films to his credit, a pundit on the BBC's ***Question Time***, a newspaper columnist and also a professional wrestler with the ring name of **Leon Aris**.

His was also the voice of many an advertising campaign, the man who told viewers that milk had ***"a lotta bottle"***, that a loaf of bread had ***"nowt tekken out"*** and that ***"Tetley make tea bags that make tea"***.

His first major role was as the bullying games master Mr Sugden in Barry Hines' iconic film *Kes*, which was being directed by Ken Loach. Hines suggested Glover (who was still a schoolmaster) for the part, and Loach asked Brian to improvise a scene in which he breaks up a fight between schoolchildren.

"I just did what I did in the playground," he revealed later. "I picked out two kids, and I banged their heads together." Glover's acting career had started...

Glover was only sixty-three when he died of a brain tumour in 1997, but he is still fondly remembered, and there are many Yorkshiremen who can cheerfully quote lines from ***Kes***, ***Porridge*** and ***An American Werewolf in London*** among many other productions which he illuminated. Brian Glover once said in an interview that, ***"In this game, acting, you play to your strengths. And my strength is as a bald-headed, rough-talking Yorkshireman."***

**Richard II** starved to death in **Pontefract Castle** in the February of 1400. A rather bad example of Yorkshire hospitality. He was only just thirty-three, and had been deposed by **Henry IV** the year before. Richard was tall, good-looking and intelligent, but was burdened with what historians believe to have been ***'personality disorders'***. He was also burdened by the highly ambitious **Henry of Bolingbroke**, the son of English hero **John of Gaunt**. It was Bolingbroke who usurped the throne and who became Henry IV.

For many years the rumour was that Richard had died from an axe wound to the head, but when his elaborate tomb in Westminster Abbey was opened many centuries later, **no damage to the skull was found.** Starvation seemed to be the cause of his demise.

Yorkshire folk have always had a soft spot for another King Richard, this time **Richard III**, who died on the battlefield of **Bosworth** in 1485, betrayed by many of his own lords and their sections of his army. He was the last English king to die in battle. Richard was succeeded by **Henry VII**, but was brought up largely at **Middleham Castle** in **Wensleydale** in North Yorkshire.

At Middleham, the young lad (he was born in 1452) was under the tutelage of his cousin, Richard Neville, the sixteenth Earl of Warwick, a noted fighter.

Richard endowed many churches and colleges, and was particularly well-loved and respected in the City of York. His Council of the North greatly improved conditions for those living in Northern England, and particularly in Yorkshire.

Richard was not only put to his books, but would exercise daily in sword-fighting skills, particularly with the broadsword, to the extent where the musculature of one side of his body was slightly larger than the other – which gave rise to Shakespeare's grotesque figure of the ***'crook-backed king'***, a gross representation of the truth.

He was the last king of the House of York.

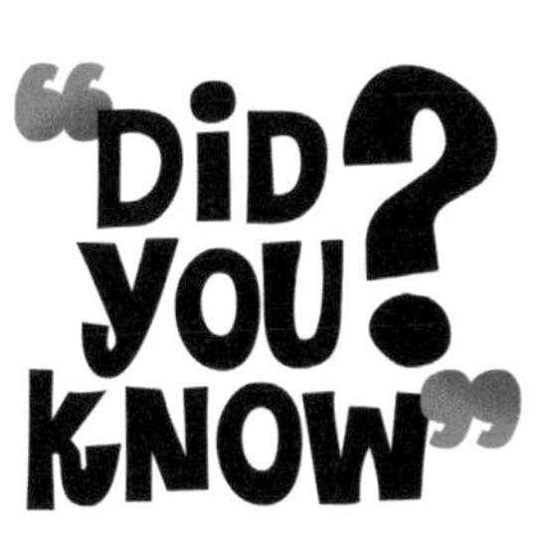


*There is a wild and remote feel to* **Cragg Vale**, *which is a very deep and very long side valley that leads up from Mytholmroyd toward Blackstone Edge and the border with Greater Manchester.*

It is still densely wooded, and in the 1760s the area was the base of the notorious **Cragg Vale Coiners**, a murderous and cunning bunch of rogues who made a very profitable living from clipping the edges from golden guinea coins and who then used the gold to imitate Portuguese coins, which at that time were, oddly enough, still recognised as legal tender.

Bell House, high above Cragg Vale, was the home of the ringleader of this unsavoury bunch, one **'*King*' David Hartley.**

He was eventually tracked down, tried and found guilty of tampering with the king's coinage, and was executed. He is buried, with other members of his family, in **Heptonstall churchyard**.

# YORKSHIRE GREATS

He was called the **Railway King**, but **George Hudson** had humble beginnings. He was born in 1800, the fifth son of a farmer, in **Scrayingham** in the old East Riding of Yorkshire. After a rudimentary education, George was apprenticed to a firm of drapers in York. He did well, and eventually was given a share in the business, which prospered mightily.

George also had the good sense to marry the daughter of the boss and to frequently attend the bedside of his dying great-uncle Matthew Botrill, who bequeathed him £30,000 in his will. And that, in 1827, was an astonishing sum of money. From being a Dissenter by religion George now decided to become a member of the High Church, and in politics was a right-wing Tory.

In 1833 there was talk of constructing a railway line from York to Leeds, and Mr Hudson was, perhaps inevitably, the largest shareholder in the company created to push the work forward. In the next fifteen years, Hudson's wealth and influence grew – and grew. It was his business acumen that caused the amalgamation of several smaller railway companies into the **Midland Railway**, and he was the man pulling a lot of strings as the Victorian ***'railway mania'*** took hold.

He was made **Lord Mayor of York** in 1837, the first of three occasions when he held the post, was elected as an **MP** (for Sunderland) in 1845, and purchased **Newby Hall** as his country seat. The house, which stands between Ripon and Thirsk, was rebuilt as **Baldersby Hall**.

And then came ruin. The man who watched over thousands of miles of railway lines was implicated in a serious fraud in the accounts of The Eastern Railway, and was also said to have bribed fellow Members of Parliament. When the general election of 1859 came around, George was rejected by his supporters. Tainted, he spent most of the rest of his years (he died in 1871) wandering on the continent, and living on small annuities granted by his depleted circles of friends.

George and his wife Florence had four children, one of whom, John, was killed in the Indian Mutiny.

There is a **Hudson House** in York (on the site of the old York and Midland Railway terminus), and also a **George Hudson Street**. He was undoubtedly the 'father' of the English railway system, with through-ticketing and sensible routes and timetables, but he was also the architect of his own downfall.

Because George Hudson had that trait that is rare in Yorkshiremen. Greed.

Today, the North Yorkshire Moors Railway, with its HQ and terminus in Pickering, still runs its celebrated steam train services on the track commissioned by George Hudson.

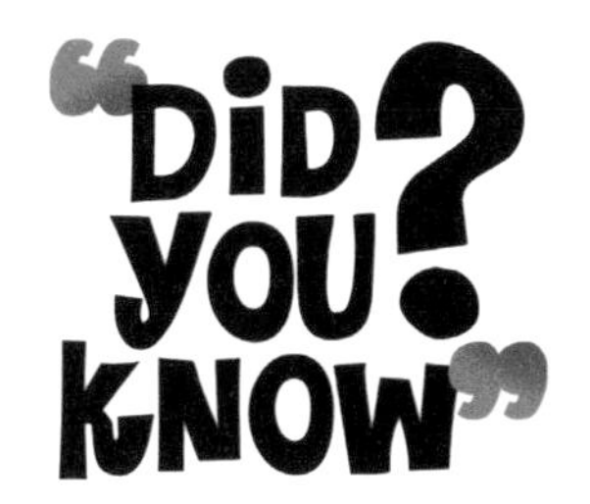

## But didn't Robin Hood come from Nottinghamshire?

Not if you believe a lot of Yorkshire legend, where it is claimed that he was born in either **York**, or **Wakefield**, or even somewhere near (obviously enough) **Robin Hood's Bay**. The place with the strongest association, however, is **Loxley**, near **Sheffield**, where he is mentioned as first seeing the light of day in the ***Sloane Manuscript*** of about 1600. He is said to be buried in the grounds of **Kirklees Priory**. He has many associations with **Barnsdale** and the old Barnsdale Forest, just north of Doncaster.

Today's image of Robin Hood is influenced by Sir Walter Scott's best-selling novel *Ivanhoe* first published in 1819. Sir Walter had visited Conisbrough Castle and set most of the novel's action there.

According to legend, Robin made the Bishop of Hereford dance a merry jig around a massive oak in Skelbrooke Park, near Wentbridge, after the prelate had made disparaging remarks about the outlaws. The place is now known as Bishop's Tree Root.

Nearby **Campsall Church** is said to be where **Robin** and **Maid Marion** were married, and there are many other tales from this part of Yorkshire that have Hood links. Not to mention, of course, **Robin Hood Airport**, at **Finningley,** near **Doncaster**, which was – until decommissioning by the RAF in 1996 – one of the pre-eminent air force bases in Britain. Maybe the site of Robin Hood Airport in South Yorkshire isn't as far-fetched as it might at first seem?

**The St Leger Stakes** is a Group One flat horse race, run annually in September in Doncaster which is open to both colts and fillies. It is the final of the **English Triple Crown**, and comes after the **2000 Guineas** and **The Derby**. It is the oldest of the British five Classics, and the last to be run.

The Leger is run over a course of one mile, six furlongs and 132 yards, or, if you prefer, 2,937 metres.

The annual event was devised by **Anthony St Leger**, and first run in 1776, on **Cantley Common**, near **Doncaster**. The winner was a filly called **Allabaculia** (the jockey was one John Singleton), and she was owned by another local landowner, the **Marquess of Rockingham** – he of the family whose business interests included making fine bone china.

A year after that first race, a committee meeting decided that it should be made an annual event, and named it after Mr St Leger. It was moved to its present racecourse site in 1778.

On a few occasions, and for various reasons, the race has been run at other locations – during both WWI and WWII the Leger moved to Newmarket for a couple of years, and most recently it went to York, in 2006, while the Doncaster course underwent extensive re-building and refurbishment.

The leading jockey, with nine winning horses in a period between 1821 and 1846, is **Bill Scott**, and **His Grace The Duke of Hamilton** remains the leading owner, with seven wins between 1786 and 1814.

**Pontefract Racecourse** is the longest continuous racing circuit in the country, just a tad short of two miles and one furlong. The precise length, from the good people at Pontefract, is two miles and 125 yards. It is a left-handed course, with a home straight of two furlongs.

**Yorkshire has the greatest number of racecourses in the UK,** and apart from Doncaster and Pontefract you may also join enthusiasts and go racing at Beverley, Wetherby, Ripon, York, Catterick and Redcar.

At Redcar, part of the course is a straight mile long – the only stretch of course in the UK that is straight as well as level.

He's a forgotten name today, but **Albert Arthur Humbles** was an English cyclist who set the world endurance record for the sport back in 1932, covering no less than 32,007 miles – that's an average of over 100 miles a day for each of the 300 days he rode, and in 1933 he entered ***The Golden Book of Cycling*** as ***the greatest long-distance cyclist in the world.***

Sadly, however, **records are made to be broken,** and Humbles' feat was soon bettered. He then had the sense to move to Whitby, and to open a cycling shop on Bridge Street. He was born in 1911, but **there seems to be no record of when the man died *... perhaps readers may help?***

**William Bradley** was once know as the **Yorkshire Giant**, and was Britain's tallest man. William, born in **Market Weighton**, was a full stone when he was born in 1787, and was no less than twenty-seven stones when he died in 1820. There were few occupations open to him, so he made a living for some time, touring with a group of itinerant fairground showmen, where visitors would see him as one of the ***'exhibits'***.

He was seven feet nine inches tall. All his clothing had to be specially made for him – his stockings were nearly four feet long. William's walking stick was said to be far taller than the height of an average man.

He once appeared before **King George III** who was so impressed with William's size and amiability that he gave him a gold chain as a souvenir. After his death he was buried secretly and in the dead of night, so that body-snatchers would not violate his grave, but he was later re-interred in the security of All Saints' Church, where there is a tablet to his memory.

Strangely enough, for a man of his size, he was said to be only a moderate eater, and when he died, it was of consumption – today's TB.

A wooden stature of William (carved from an English oak log by **Malcolm MacLachlan**) stands in the centre of Market Weighton, and William's house, on York Road, is nearby. It had to be built specially for him, with rooms that would accommodate his standing up with ease. On the wall of the house is an ancient plaque showing the size of the shoes that he wore. They measure fifteen inches in length and five and

Record Breakers

three-quarter inches in width. Market Weighton citizens celebrate Giant Bradley Day each year in May.

William Bradley would have found it difficult indeed to fit into **Yorkshire's smallest house,** which is in Whitby, by the harbourside, and which used to be an old pumping station, and he would have found it nigh-impossible to fit into the **smallest snug bar in Britain,** which is in the Minerva pub in Hull, and which just accommodates two normally-sized persons.

**The highest pub in Britain is the Tan Hill Inn, in Swaledale, between Reeth and Richmond, and which sits on a ridge at 1,732 feet above sea level. In 1586, the traveller William Camden notes "a solitary inn", but the present building dates from the seventeenth century.**

It was recently used by the Everest double glazing firm in a series of adverts promoting their products – the company had used the location before in their campaigns. And the inn is said to be haunted by the ghost of a former much-loved landlady, **Susan Peacock**, who reigned over the pumps for many years from 1903. Susan clearly embraced the modern technology of the day, and she made several very popular broadcasts on the new-fangled wireless in the 1930s about life at the inn and its solitary situation. As a result, hundreds of punters turned up to enjoy the Tan Hill's hospitality.

***The inn is frequently snowed in and cut off to traffic in bad weather conditions in winter.***

The late Poet Laureate, **Sir John Betjeman**, called **Huddersfield railway station *"the most splendid in England"***. It was designed in the neo-classical style by **Joseph Pigott Pritchett** and built in 1846-50.

The station is on St George's Square, and in front of the building is a large statue of **Harold Wilson** (unveiled by Tony Blair in 1999), remarkable because it omits a vital part of Wilson's 'public image' – his pipe. In private, however, he was rather more partial to a good cigar.

**The eminent architectural historian Sir Nikolaus Pevsner also called Huddersfield station *"One of the best early railway stations in England"*.**

Harold Wilson, or Lord Wilson of Rievaulx as he later became, was born in **Huddersfield** in 1916. He became Labour leader in 1963, on the death of Hugh Gaitskell, and won the general election the following year. He lost the subsequent 1970 election, but was returned to power in 1974, before finally resigning as Prime Minister two years later. He remained a serving MP until 1983, and died in 1995.

The sculpture is by Ian Walters.

**The National Railway Museum in York is the biggest museum of its kind in the world,** with over a hundred locomotives of all shapes and sizes on display, as well as other rolling stock and artefacts and railway memorabilia of every kind. It offers extensive research facilities.

The Yorkshire private house with 365 rooms is **Wentworth Woodhouse**, near **Rotherham**, once the stately home of the **Marquesses of Rockingham**, and then the **Earls Fitzwilliam**.

***It has the longest frontage of any home in Europe, twice as long as Buckingham Palace.***

Built in the 1730s, the huge estate stood over the Barnsley seam of coal, which provided the Fitzwilliam family wealth over many generations.

When Labour came to power as the 1939-45 war ended, Manny Shinwell was appointed Minister of Fuel and Power, and, in an act of unprecedented vindictiveness, ordered that the newly nationalised National Coal Board should carry out mining operations right up to the mansion's back door.

The house later became a training college, and is now once again in private hands. ***Wentworth Woodhouse is emphatically not open to the public***, although there is limited access to the grounds, which contain many splendid follies, one of which is a monument to **Admiral August Keppel**, the seaman who was court-martialled, and then acquitted. Keppel was a close friend of the Rockinghams.

The **Bingley Five-Rise Locks** on the **Leeds-Liverpool Canal** are the steepest in the UK. Opened on 12th March 1774, it was a major engineering feat of its day, with a gradient of about one in five – fifty-nine feet, two inches over a distance of 320 feet – and when the locks were first used for traffic, a crowd of 30,000 turned out to watch. A barge could be lifted through the locks in twenty-eight minutes. The smaller **Three Rise** opened at the same time, just over 300 yards further down.

Each of the five chambers is fourteen feet wide, and each gate consists of two half-gates of just over seven feet wide, hinged at each side of the canal, and pointed upstream when closed – water pressure therefore keeps it tightly closed. **The intermediate and bottom gates are the tallest in the country,** and because the canal is a popular tourist attraction, a full-time lock-keeper is required to assist traffic to travel up and down the system. **The structure is Grade I listed.**

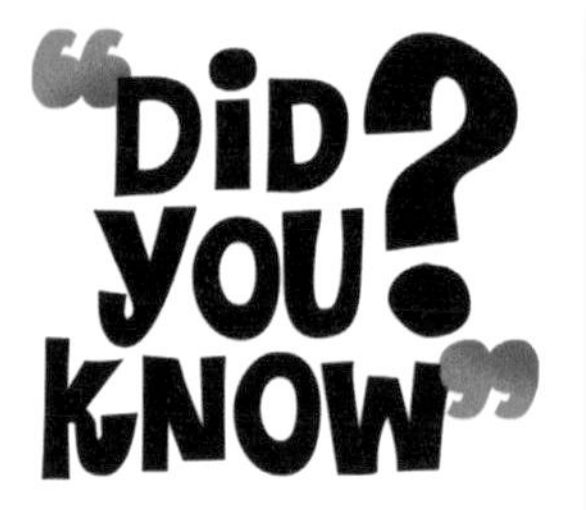


**The Standedge Tunnel**, on the Huddersfield Narrow Canal, **is the longest of its kind in Britain – and also the highest.** It runs under the Pennines from Marsden in Yorkshire, and is 14,499 feet long. **At its deepest point it is 636 feet underground.**

Opened on 4th April 1811, there had been many trials and tribulations en route, with several engineers giving conflicting opinions on how the project should go ahead. **Benjamin Outram** was the first consulting engineer, but it was the legendary **Thomas Telford** who finally brought the construction to a successful conclusion.

One of the problems with the tunnel is that – to cut costs – for most of its distance the canal was made wide enough for only one boat at a time. There is no towpath alongside the waterway, and so **all the barges had to be 'legged' along its length,** with the bargeman and any helpers flat on their backs on the roof of the barge, physically 'walking' along the rock and brick above them.

Professional ***'leggers'*** were paid one shilling and sixpence (7½p) for each barge they walked through the tunnel – with a load on board it took a full three hours, and one hour twenty minutes if the barge was empty.

The Standedge Tunnel was purchased by the **Huddersfield and Manchester Railway Company** in 1846, and actually proved to be very useful when they and their successors (chiefly the London and North Western Railway) built a trio of rail tunnels running parallel with that for the canal – a series of cross-tunnels (or adits) at strategic locations meant that the waste and spoil could be carried off down the waterway. The three tunnels are still maintained, but only the 1894 one carries through-traffic today. It is the shortest of the tunnels, but it still runs underground for three miles and sixty yards. **Network Rail** are considering the re-opening of both of its companions, in order to raise the capacity of cross-country traffic.

# YORKSHIRE GREATS

**Giggleswick School, near Settle** in North Yorkshire, was the alma mater of journalist, author, TV presenter, ***Countdown*** host, and ferret-wrangler, **Richard Whiteley**, where a new 288-seater theatre is named after him. The ***Tatler Schools Guide*** for 2011 reveals that since 2002, an astonishing 100 per cent of theatre studies pupils have achieved either A or B grades. The *Guide* goes on: ***"Art is good too, and eccentricities are happily accommodated."*** It adds that the school, known familiarly as Gigg, has pupils that are polite ***"and – in the nicest possible way – charmingly unsophisticated, compared with their world-weary urban contemporaries."***

At the time of his death **Whiteley proudly held the record for the most number of hours of appearances on British television – over 10,000.** The only person who could claim more was Carole Hersee, the little girl who appeared on the BBC's iconic Test Card F. Because Richard would appear on ***Countdown*** on Channel 4, and then be seen presenting Yorkshire Television's evening news programme ***Calendar*** only a few minutes later, **some wag nicknamed him *"Twice nightly Whiteley"*.**

**Ever self-deprecating, the man himself observed that that should really be *"Once yearly, nearly"*.**

The much-loved and equally much-missed Richard (born in Bradford and for many years the Mayor of Wetwang) was the first face to be seen when Channel 4 started broadcasting on 2nd

November 1982, and his association with the programme only ended with his death in June 2005. When his memorial service was held on 10th November 2005, York Minster was packed with thousands of Richard's family, friends and fans. His co-host on ***Countdown***, **Carol Vorderman**, paid tribute by saying that, had Whiteley been present, ***"he would have greeted you all, one by one, would have shaken every one of you by the hand – and would have wanted a photograph taken."***

Britain's first-ever air show (only the second in the world) was held on Doncaster Racecourse in 1909, only months after a similar exposition at Rheims in France. All the world's leading aviators were present, among them Wilbur Wright, Louis Bleriot and Samuel Cody, from the USA, who gave an added entertainment bonus to the crowd when he was granted British citizenship on the racecourse turf, and signed his naturalisation papers as the band played ***The Star-Spangled Banner*** and then ***God Save the King***. Unfortunately, later in the day he crashed his plane while taxiing.

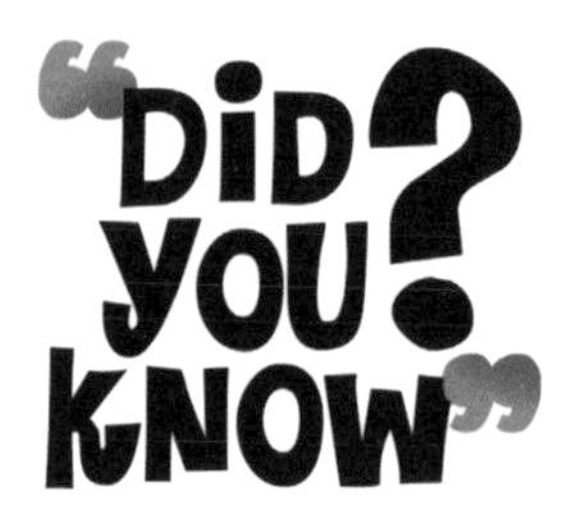


**The Doncaster Air Museum** (on the site of part of what was the local RAF base, and about half a mile away from the racecourse) has a poster commemorating the airshow. **It is estimated that 100,000 people (and more) attended the event, many arriving on special train services.**

**The Grand Hotel in Scarborough** was designed by **Hull-born architect Cuthbert Brodrick** (who also designed Leeds' Town Hall and the Mechanic's Institute building that now houses the city's museum) and is the only ***'calendar'*** hotel in Europe.

It has four massive towers (to represent the four seasons), twelve floors for the months of the year, fifty-two chimneys for the weeks, and – when it first opened – 365 bedrooms, one for each day of the year.

**YORKSHIRE GREATS**

Broderick further embellished the symbolism of the building, because it is in the shape of a 'V', a loyal nod to his monarch, Victoria.

**The hotel's other claim to fame is that it has not one but three blue plaques on its exterior walls.** One is for the novelist Anne Brontë, **who died in a house on the site in 1849,** the second is to mark the contributions of RAF trainees to the wartime effort **– the aircraftmen were billeted at the Grand after 1939 –** and the third is for the remarkable building itself.

The Grand opened in 1867, and was then one of the largest hotels in the world. It is built of local bricks made in nearby Hunmanby, and is now Grade II listed. In the postwar period, the hotel was owned by the **Butlin's Holiday Camp** group.

GUESS WHO

**Charles Dickens'** third novel, ***The Life and Adventures of Nicholas Nickleby***, features the squalid Dotheboys Hall, an educational establishment for young men, and somewhere near to **Greta Bridge** in North Yorkshire. It is ruled by the appalling, tyrannical and one-eyed headmaster **Wackford Squeers**, and young Nicholas goes there as a teacher. He is revolted by the conditions of the place. Dickens undoubtedly heard of the reputation of some of the real-life Yorkshire 'schools' of his day.

The novel began life as a serialisation in 1838. Squeers advertised his establishment as having ***"no extras, no vacations"***.

Earlier in 1838, Dickens and Hablot Browne, the illustrator for the book, travelled to Yorkshire to see some of the boarding schools for themselves. In the preface to his novel Dickens observes that Yorkshire schoolmasters are

*"Traders in the avarice, indifference or imbecility of parents, and the helplessness of children; ignorant, sordid brutal men to whom few considerate persons would have entrusted the board and lodgings of a horse or a dog; they formed the worthy cornerstone of a structure, which, for absurdity and a magnificent high-minded laissez-aller of neglect, has rarely been exceeded in this world."*

During their short visit the two men visited **Bowes Academy** run by the notorious **William Shaw**. He had previously been prosecuted for neglect – boys in his care had starved, some had gone blind and some had died. He was still allowed to run his Academy. Dickens got some of the names for his characters by wandering in the nearby churchyards where Shaw's victims were buried.

Over the years, Dickens returned many times to Yorkshire to perform readings from his works before hugely enthusiastic audiences. He went to (among many other locations) Leeds, Sheffield and Hull. He was firm friends with a Malton family, the Smithsons, whom he visited on many occasions, and it is said that he based the counting house of Scrooge the miser on one of their offices in Malton's Chancery Lane. The church bells, which feature so prominently in *A Christmas Carol*, were based on those of St Leonard's in Malton, and triggered Dickens' fertile imagination.

**Mr Spenlow, in *David Copperfield*, is said to be based on Charles Smithson, and Sairey Gamp, in *Martin Chuzzlewit*, is based on the Smithsons' housekeeper of the time.** Dickens also visited the churchyards of Scarborough and Filey, **and wrote movingly of the number of men and women buried there after being drowned off the coast.**

## Guess Who

**Bram (Abraham) Stoker** was an Irishman who spent his first seven years as an invalid, and then made a splendid recovery – in his student years in Dublin he was respected as something of an athlete. He met **Sir Henry Irving** when the actor went on a tour of Irish theatres. Irving had enjoyed a favourable review from Stoker on his production of ***Hamlet***. In 1879 Stoker and his new wife **Florence**, a famous society beauty of her day, moved to London, where Bram's long and fruitful business association with Irving began, but he also started to write novels, the first of which was ***The Snake's Pass*** in 1890. ***Dracula*** was to follow in 1897.

Stoker had spent several holidays in or near Whitby, on the North Yorkshire coast, and on one of them had seen a ship, the *Dmitri*, run aground after a violent storm. No surprise then, that in his famous book, a Russian ship, the *Demeter*, runs aground at Whitby, but in the novel the crew and any passengers have mysteriously vanished, and the only body recovered is the vessel's captain, who is lashed to the helm. His log is found, and it proves to be an account of the voyage, and some highly mysterious happenings. And then a large black dog is seen leaping from the ship...

It is said that Stoker had spent many hours in Whitby's public library, poring over their collection of folklore and legend, and that it was here that he found the name of

DREAMS
LOVE LOST
TAKE ME

**Dracula**, and the story of the legendary **Vlad the Impaler**. Since its first sensational publication ***Dracula*** has never been out of print, and has been turned into countless films, TV dramas and radio plays. And it has done no harm at all to Whitby's tourist trade.

*Whitby has something of a literary reputation – could it be something in the sea air?*

Apart from **Bram Stoker**, among other famous writers associated with the town is **Wilkie Collins**, who worked on his novel ***No Name*** while visiting with his companion **Caroline Graves**, who was his muse for ***The Woman in White***.

Then there's

***Storm Jameson, who was born in the town...***

and **James Russell Lowell**, who was American Ambassador to the Court of St James in the 1890s, also a writer of some note.

***Mrs Elizabeth Gaskell sets part of her Sylvia's Lovers in the town...***

and it is also referenced by **A S Byatt** in ***Possession...***

***...and by Kim Wilkins in The Resurrectionists***

and there are more...

**Whitby Abbey** which stands imperiously on the headland was founded in AD 657, and was the location of the **Synod of Whitby** in 664. The meeting was to determine whether or not the Roman calendar should be used in determining the date of **Easter**, or if the Celtic dating was preferable. The Roman calendar prevailed, and the Celtic influence in the Church was on the wane from that point.

The original abbey was **destroyed in a notoriously bloody and vindictive Viking raid in AD 867,** and it wasn't until the eleventh century that a Norman knight, **William de Percy,** came trotting past, and was inspired to rebuild the whole thing.

The building continued to be an influence on the town until Henry VIII, the king who was always chopping and changing, forced the **Act of Dissolution** on the monasteries. Yorkshire was hard hit, for it was home to a large concentration of these monastic houses – **Fountains, Rievaulx, Mount Grace** and **Roche** to name only a few.

# YORKSHIRE GREATS

**Sandal is a peculiarly Yorkshire word – Sandal Beat in Doncaster, Kirk Sandal, Sandal Magna ... it derives from the early Scandinavian word *sandr*, meaning sand or gravel, and *healh*, a meadow.**

**The Crusaders** are said to have brought the liquorice root to Yorkshire, and particularly to the area around **Pontefract**, while Spanish monks also brought it into Yorkshire, where they used the plant for medicinal purposes at **Rievaulx Abbey**, near Thirsk. But it was in the deep sandy soil around Pontefract (from the Latin ***Ponte Fractus***, meaning broken bridge) that it took root, and the hugely popular little liquorice sweeties, named **Pontefract** (or Pomfret) **cakes**, are still made there to this day, though sadly not in as great a number as of yore. There's even a poem about the liquorice fields, and (perhaps unsurprisingly) it is by the late Poet Laureate, **Sir John Betjeman**.

*By the liquorice fields of Pontefract*
*My Love and I did meet,*
*And many a burdened Liquorice bush*
*Was blooming round our feet;*
*Red hair she had, and golden skin,*
*Her sulky lips were shaped for sin,*
*Her sturdy legs were flannel slack'd,*
*The strongest legs in Pontefract.*

"Well I Never

**Malham Cove**, a huge naturally curving amphitheatre-shaped limestone cliff formation is one of the natural wonders of the world, and is some 260 feet (80 metres) high and 984 feet (300 metres) wide.

The top of the cliff is a vast, deeply eroded limestone pavement, and has been attracting visitors for centuries.

Many more have turned up in their thousands since the stunning feature was used as a backdrop for scenes in **Harry Potter and the Deathly Hallows** – Harry camped out on the limestone pavement, and there were also views of Gordale Scar and Malham Tarn.

Describing the Cove back in 1779, **Adam Walker** observed that:

**"This beautiful rock is like the age-tinted wall of a prodigious castle; the stone is very white, and from the walls hang various shrubs and vegetables, which – with the tints from the bog water – gives it a variety that I never before saw so pleasing in a plain rock."**

Little has changed since then.

Divers and pot-holers have (so far) explored over a mile of cave passages, entering from a passage at the base of the Cove.

**The valley was formed at the end of the last ice age, when the ground was completely frozen, and when things began to warm up some 12,000 years ago (it is estimated) the ground thawed and the river in the valley below the Cove went underground, leaving it roughly as we see it today.**

On the west side of the cliff face are some 400 irregular stone steps, which form part of the **Pennine Way**.

***The Pennine Way Trail starts far south of Malham, in Edale in Derbyshire, and goes as far north as the Cheviots, some 268 miles of spectacular upland walking – but nothing takes the breath away for Way Walkers so much as Malham Cove.***

*Yorkshire Tea is made by Taylor's of Harrogate, and among tea-drinking superstitions you can find that*:

If the lid to the teapot is left off, a stranger will arrive bearing bad news.

A pair of teaspoons left accidentally together in a saucer means a wedding. Or a pregnancy.

Rather sweet, this one – bubbles on the surface of a cup of tea mean that someone will be getting a lot of kisses.

Stirring the tea anti-clockwise in the pot is sure to stir up trouble

To spill a little of the tea while you are making it is a good omen (unless of course someone has just spread a fresh white linen tablecloth!)

Few snooker players will confess it, but their game is as rife with superstitions as is the world of the theatre. And when the top players in the game descend yearly on **Sheffield's Crucible Theatre**, the place is a hive of superstitious activity, according to those in the know backstage. "They nearly all have various rituals" an insider told the author …

"… it's amazing – wearing the right colour socks, not wearing new shoes, having a particular cue in their hands, not saying this, not saying that. Not whistling before a match … not that, as you'd expect, any of them will admit to anything so daft and inexplicable. It's all for good luck … "

The present 'castle' on **Castle Hill** in **Almondbury** isn't actually a castle at all, but is really a tower, built in 1898 to celebrate **Queen Victoria's Diamond Jubilee**. The view from the parapets is stunning, and from it you can see for miles, right over the village of Almondbury below, and off to Halifax in the distance.

**The Hill itself has been occupied for over 4,000 years, and the Brigantes, the tribe of the area, set up an Iron Age fort, and there are remains of vast ramparts around the hilltop.**

It is assumed that the **Romans** cleared out the original occupants. Later, the **Normans**, in the shape of the **de Laci family**, built a sturdy castle on the hill, which was started in the 1140s and existed up until around 1340. A pair of medieval wells have been discovered by archaeologists..

But, like a lot of hills and mounds with prehistoric evidence, the hill has both mystical and magical associations.

A fearsome dragon is said to have lived directly under the 900-foot-high hill, and he guarded an immense golden treasury. There are also supposed to be no less than five tunnels leading from deep inside the hill and the dragon's lair to various houses and communities in the area.

Not only that, the site has been put forward as a candidate for the location of the mythical **King Arthur's Camelot**.

The Devil gets out and about a bit in Yorkshire. The Devil's Punchbowl is the name given to the magnificent **Hole of Horcum**, an enormous depression that can be found at the highest part of the North York Moors, near to the Pickering to Whitby road. At this point, travellers are 1,490 feet above the sea.

Folklore has two explanations for its origin. The first is that the Devil bent and scooped out the land in a moment of idleness – a nearby bend in the road is known locally as the Devil's Elbow – and the second is that the giant Wade dug up handfuls of earth which he then used to make nearby Blakey Topping and Wade's Causeway.

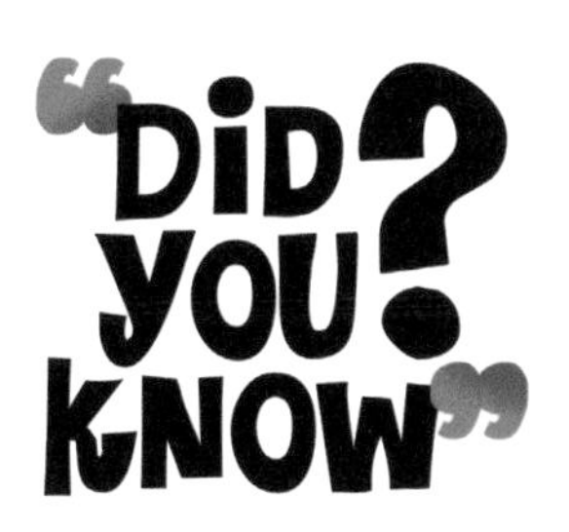


According to legend Old Nick also built **Dibble's Bridge** near Burnsall in Wharfedale, over a stream called the Dib. It is claimed that he performed the task for a medieval shoemaker called **Ralph Calvert**, of Thorpe-sub-Montem, although quite why he should spend his time in this engineering feat for a humble cobbler is not known.

**Hull skippers believed in "A Friday sail will always fail", and refused to leave port on that day.**

There was an old Yorkshire saying that ***went: "Friday flit, short sit"***, meaning that it was unlucky to move house on that day, because you would not reside long in your new home.

However, in Pagan times, Friday was considered to be ***a day of excellent omen.***

In Yorkshire when the bride returned to her parental home after her wedding, a plate with some of the wedding cake was flung out of the window. If the plate broke, she would enjoy a long and happy future with her husband. If it didn't, things weren't going to go that well. It is not recorded what fortune befell any innocent passer-by who was hit by the flying crockery and cake.

Housewives in the county used to believe that **bread would not rise if there was a corpse nearby,** and that if they cut off both ends of a loaf, the devil would fly over the house.

**Magpies** are also thought of as ill omens. In Yorkshire the bird is associated with witchcraft, and if one is seen, you should make a sign of the cross, then doff your cap or any headgear. In parts of the county it was advised that the observer should make a noise like the bird's partner.

There was a Methodist belief in the north of the county that Fridays were particularly unlucky, and not just when they happened to coincide with the number thirteen.

This is apparently because of a legend that, on his way to Calvary, Christ's face was deliberately splashed with a wet garment by a woman washing. He cursed her and ***"everyone who shall wash on this day hereafter"***. A Whitby belief goes that clothes hung out to dry on a Friday ***"shall be taken down spotted by blood"***.

**In the days of the old bathing machines at Scarborough, an attendant was hugely reluctant to take them out for swimmers on a Friday *"because that's the day that most accidents happen."***

One of the bells at **Dewsbury's All Saints' Minster Church** is known as **Black Tom**, and weighs thirteen hundredweight. It bears the inscription:

> ***"I shall be heard, if treated just,***
> ***When you are mouldering in dust".***

Every Christmas Eve this tenor bell is rung slowly, one chime for every year since Christ's birth, and the peal ends on the stroke of midnight. The origins of the custom date back to around 1434, when **Sir Thomas Soothill**, the then Lord of the local manor, and apparently cursed with an appalling temper, murdered a young servant boy and hid his body in the nearby Forge Dam. Or disposed of it in the furnace of the local blacksmith, according to another account. Sir Thomas, full of remorse at some point later, endowed the bell.

> **The medieval theory was that the Devil died when Christ was born, and that a bell chiming five times would announce that he had passed away and that he would not trouble the townsfolk in the coming year.**

The knell for a man's death was four rings four times, and that for a woman three rings three times, so it seems that Beelzebub got an extra one. The toll for the years since Christ's birth then follows, and that starts before ten pm, so that the timing of the final 'dong' is perfect. The ceremony is known as **Tolling the Devil's Knell**, and when this custom was featured on a set of Post Office commemorative stamps back in 1986, requests for first day covers came in from all around the world. Designed by **Lynda Gray** in the style of ancient book illustrations, no less than ten million stamps were sold.

There are few people who have had a species of moth named after them, but **Ursula Southeil** (or Southall) has that honour. You'll know her better as **Old Mother Shipton**. The moth, ***Callistege mi***, apparently has a pattern that looks like a hag's head on each wing.

Ursula, **who was reputedly hideously ugly,** was a prophetess and soothsayer and was born somewhere around 1488. She died in 1561, **and her book of insights into the future** did not appear until almost a century later.

It contained a great many predictions about Yorkshire, but did not – as everyone assumes – say anything at all about the world coming to an end on a specific date.

Ursula was born in **Knaresborough**, says a 1684 edition of her book, and in a rather strange place – the cave that now bears her name. The book also claims that she married a local carpenter, **Toby Shipton**, in York in 1512, and was always known for her telling of fortunes.

**She has been an inspiration for many occultists ever since, and her fame is not confined to Yorkshire or the UK, for her name has continually been linked to strange and often tragic events.**

She has certainly put her home town firmly on the map, and in addition to that moth, there's a pub in Knaresborough named after her.

Yorkshire superstitions are many – and varied. And a lot of them have maritime connections. In **Filey**, **Flamborough** and **Scarborough** it was thought to be horribly unlucky to say the words ***'pig'*** or ***'rabbit'*** to a sailor, and particularly to a fisherman. The Flamborough lads never used the word ***'last'*** when hauling in their pots and nets, and would say ***'end line'*** or ***'end crab pot'*** instead. The men were not alone, for their womenfolk thought it would bring bad luck if they wound the wool for the jerseys they were knitting by the light of a lamp.

**In Runswick Bay, the locals believed that the caves in the cliffs were inhabited by their own special Hob, or goblin, and that the creature could cure whooping cough. They took their children along to the south of the bay, and would call out**

***"Hob – Hole – Hob!***
***My bairn's getten t'kink-cough,***
***tak't off, tak't off."***

Victorian writers have left accounts of the Runswick Bay youngsters going up onto the cliff during a storm, and dancing while chanting

***"Souther wind, souther, and blow***
***fether home t'mother."***

They also mention the practice of sacrificing a moggie if the fishing fleet returned home safely after a bad storm. Lucky for the matelots, not so lucky for the cat. And it was believed that bad fishing (and worse) would be had if a man saw a female while walking down to his boat in the morning. If he did, he'd turn on his heels, and return home.

In his *Times* obituary of 11th February 2004, **Richard Henry Piers Butler**, seventeenth Viscount Mountgarret, was described as ***"impetuous and irascible"***. His Lordship was certainly a one-off, and a genuine Yorkshire eccentric who made his indelible mark in many fields. He came into 10,000 acres of North Yorkshire land (and another 25,000 in Scotland), a good few ancient mines, and a lot of buildings with the letter M in stone somewhere on their roofs and porches, surmounted by the Viscount's coronet.

**Born in November 1936, he inherited one of the finest estates in the north of England, and he ran it according to his own rules.**

He was a particularly successful President of Yorkshire County Cricket Club, **although he wasn't a particularly good cricketer himself when younger.** But in the troubled 1980s, Mountgarret poured a lot of oil on choppy waters, and calmed down a lot of tempers – **to the surprise of many who knew him.**

Elsewhere, there were drains on his purse, not least in two costly divorce case and disputes with his sister and his own children. One of the things that went was the **Lordship of the Manor of Stanbury**, a title belonging to a place not thirty miles from Mountgarret's home.

He revealed that he didn't care a jot about selling the title, because he hadn't got a clue where it was.

Educated at Eton and then Sandhurst, Viscount Mountgarret was rather deaf when he left the Irish Guards in 1964 –

which may well have accounted for the incident when the noble peer took three pot-shots at a balloonist who he thought was going to accidentally land in one of his fields, which would have disturbed the nesting grouse. The balloonist, who was hit but not badly wounded, was, in fact, trying to warn Mountgarret of his descent. Two years later the same unfortunate fellow made another forced landing on the Mountgarret estate. This time his balloon was confiscated.

In 1999, a gamekeeper who had been ejected from a rent-free cottage on the estate won a goodly sum (£19,484) when a court ruled that the action had been unfair. They heard that Mountgarret had called the man

***"a bloody idiot, a bloody imbecile"***

in front of his shooting chums. But he was also, paradoxically, much liked and respected by others of his workers.

The year was not a good one for the Viscount, for he lost his hereditary seat in the Lords (he sat on the Tory benches) in the Labour reforms to that House. Among other policies, he advocated the castration of rapists if they re-offended, didn't approve of the compulsory wearing of seat-belts, and wanted hanging brought back in certain cases. He grew weary of farming, and had no time for accountants. When he died on 7th February, 2004, his son, also called Piers, succeeded to the title. He died at the wheel of his car, but had fortunately managed to bring it to a halt before a heart attack claimed him.

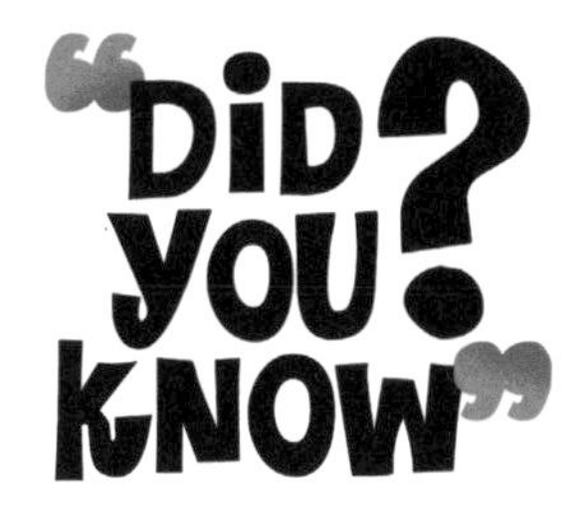


Another larger than life character, but from a couple of centuries earlier, was **Charles Waterton**, the Yorkshire naturalist and explorer. He was born at the family home of **Walton Hall**, near **Wakefield**, in 1782. The family, which could be traced back to pre-Norman Conquest times, claimed to have no fewer than eight saints in their pedigree, including **Vladimir of Russia**, **Queen Margaret of Scotland** and **Saint Thomas More**.

Waterton was fascinated by Guiana, and started travelling further afield to note the flora and fauna, and even managed to travel – in bare feet – to Brazil.

Many of the specimens that Waterton captured, had stuffed, and brought back to Yorkshire are still on display at Wakefield Museum, captivating youngsters of the twenty-first century.

Charles' interest in natural history started at school, and when he left, he almost immediately set off on an expedition to British Guiana, chiefly to look after his uncle's estates in Georgetown. He published ***Waterton's Wanderings in South America***, which thrilled schoolboys back home in Blighty. At the age of forty seven he married a young lady of eighteen, and when she died in childbirth he took to sleeping on the floor, with a wooden block as his pillow. When he died in May 1865, he was buried between two oaks on the estate.

**After he returned to Walton Hall in the early 1820s he had a nine-foot-high wall built around his remaining land and created the very first nature reserve in Britain behind it.**

PETE

Among many things which marked out **Charles Waterton** as a non-conformist were that he had his hair in a crew-cut when other styles were considered to be the norm, that he once tried to fly by jumping out of a window (he called this ***'navigating the atmosphere'*** ) and that on one occasion he left his gloves on the tip of one of the lightning conductors on the roof of St Peter's in Rome. The Pope asked him if he would kindly remove them, and Waterton cheerfully obliged.

One of his many skills was in taxidermy, and **he would often create tableaus of various animals,** lampooning contemporary politicians – and also those who he considered his enemies.

He would, it is said, imitate a dog at the dinner table, and, barking happily, **would scamper about under the table,** nipping the ankles of the assembled guests.

**Waterton Lakes**, the Canadian National Park in Alberta, is named after him, as is a **Wakefield** road, and a school.

***He was a fervent opponent of pollution in all its forms, and successfully closed down a soap-works in Wakefield that sent fumes belching into the surrounding air.***

***In the annual Knaresborough Bed Race every summer, teams of locals and visitors (six runners and one passenger) decorate special 'beds' to parade through the town.***

Today they are made of tubular steel, and are highly and eccentrically decorated. Then, when the beds have completed the parade, they are stripped to their bare components, and the race begins through the streets.

The climax comes when **the beds and the teams who propel them are required to cross the River Nidd,** and many have sunk below the surface in the attempt. The finishing line is up a muddy bank on yonder side of the river.

**In addition to the Knaresborough folk,** guest contestants over the years have included **the erstwhile Chief Scout Peter Duncan (of *Blue Peter* and *Duncan Dares* fame) comedian Rory McGrath, radio talkshow host James Whale (long a stalwart of Yorkshire Television's late night output) and representatives from Knaresborough's twin town of Bebra, in Germany.** What the German visitors make of it all is anyone's guess.

## "ah'm fair capped"

**Jemmy Hirst** is commemorated today by a rather fine pub at **Rawcliffe**, near Goole in East Yorkshire. He was born into a wealthy farming family, and there were signs that the young Jemmy was a bit, well, different when, as a lad, he kept a pet jackdaw, and then trained a hedgehog to follow him around. His eccentricity grew with the years, and some said it was brought on when he rescued his bride-to-be from a flooded river. She died after developing smallpox. Jemmy then decided to train somewhat larger animals than hitherto, and started with one of the farm bulls, whom he called **Jupiter**. The beast pulled Jemmy's carriage (which was made from wicker) from place to place, but rather slowly.

The inventive Mr Hirst decided that the conveyance would go more quickly with the **addition of sails**, and he was right. But unfortunately it went so fast that he, it and Jupiter all crashed into the window of a draper's shop in Pontefract. **He was afterwards banned from the town.**

Jemmy turned his attention to training pigs to jump hurdles, and to use them in following the local hunt.

Then King George III heard about him (*that's right, the monarch who had mental problems of his own to think about*) and invited him to London. Jemmy thanked him for the thought, but sent word that he was *too busy training otters to fish better!*

When he found time to meet the king, he wore what he'd worn to Doncaster races – a lambskin hat with a nine-foot brim, and a waistcoat made of duck feathers. One of the nobles at court was daft enough to laugh at Jemmy's attire, upon which the Yorkshireman threw the contents of a goblet into the peer's face. Jemmy observed that it had "cured the man's hysterics". Jemmy summed up George as "a plain-looking fellow", but still returned home with the gift of a few good bottles from the royal cellars.

**His will** stipulated that he be buried in his self-designed coffin, which had windows in it, and also a bell, in case he had been wrongly certified as being dead. He wanted a fiddler and a bagpiper to ***"play happy songs"*** as the cortege wended its way to his final resting place. The spoilsport of a vicar forbade the fiddler to play a single note, and told the piper that the only tune that he'd hear was ***Over the Hills and Far Away***.

**Jemmy later married his housekeeper – dressed in a toga. The ceremony was conducted in sign language. To the end of his days, in 1829 and aged ninety, Mr Hirst would give a blast on his hunting horn to summon the poor and elderly of the parish to his home for tea.**

*Jemmy would, like as not, have enjoyed the fact that he left a sovereign each to 'twelve elderly virgins' who were to follow his coffin. Only two could be found. But then, Rawcliffe was a pretty small village.*

The image of Yorkshiremen that has circulated the globe is the ***Monty Python*** sketch in which four heavily-accented blokes sit around, reminiscing about how hard their lives on the path to success have been.

Sample: First Yorkshireman:

**" ... when I was a lad, our dad used to thrash us with belts."**

Second Yorkshireman:

**"Luxury! We had to get out of the lake at three o'clock in the morning, clean the lake, eat a handful of hot gravel, go to work at the mill every day for tuppence a month, come home and Dad would beat us around the head and the neck with a broken bottle, and that were if we were LUCKY!"**

The four were played by **Graham Chapman**, **Eric Idle**, **Terry Jones** and Sheffield's own **Michael Palin**.

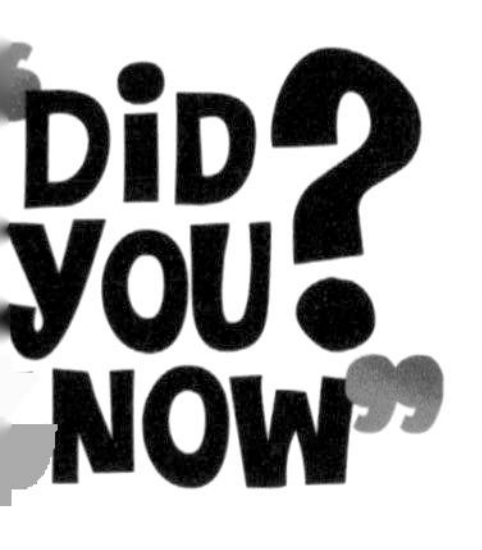


Many Yorkshire towns and cities are 'twinned' with other communities around the world, but perhaps it is **Whitby** that has the most intriguing list of civic companions. Whitby is twinned with: Anchorage in Alaska, Port Stanley in the Falkland Islands, Porirua in New Zealand, Longueuil in Quebec, Canada, Nuku'alofa in Tonga and Kauai County in Hawaii.

**The Whitby to Scarborough railway line** was one of the most scenic stretches in Britain. Opened in 1885, the spectacular views across the **North Sea** had passengers open-mouthed in appreciation – and those to the **North York Moors** were equally as fine. Small wonder, then, that someone dreamed up the idea of building a completely new town at **Ravenscar**, and registered the **Ravenscar Estate Company** in 1895. It couldn't fail, could it?

Well I Never!

**What could possibly go wrong with a town that had magnificent golf links, bracing air, moorland walks, and that vista across the ocean?** Valuable building plots were offered for sale, and the Raven Hall Hotel (in a house which once belonged to Dr Willis, who treated George III for his bouts of insanity), with its cliff terraces and hanging gardens, looked forward to a surge in trade.

Sewage facilities were put in, and drains laid. Some houses went up … and then it all staggered to a halt. The developers hadn't factored in a very simple stumbling block to the scene. Their town was going to stand 600 feet above the sea below, and there wasn't much of a beach anyway. In fact, it consists of boulders, large and small.

***The scheme never took off, and Ravenscar became the Town that Never Was.***

Ravenscar stands within the parish of **Staintondale**, and, in the 2001 census, the total population was given as a staggering 319.

Ravenscar – which featured prominently in artistic impressions as a thriving resort in a few Victorian postcards – is at the end of the **Lyke Wake Walk**, and the **Cleveland Trail** passes through it. It was intended as a rival to Scarborough. It never ever came close.

***Robin Hood's Well, at Skellow, is probably the most useless well ever.***

It was moved to the south-bound side of the **Great North Road** when road-widening was taking place, and therefore, since it has a stone base, is not a well at all. Designed by **Vanbrugh**, it was formerly near to the **River Skell**, and fine clear water bubbled up into the well itself.

A traveller in 1634 remarked on ***"tasting a cup"*** at the well, and author John Evelyn called it ***"a crystal spring"***, and described a seat and a ladle on a long iron chain.

WHITBY
ABBEY

**Whitby** is almost certainly one of the **most haunted places in Yorkshire**, and is steeped in folklore and legend.

**The first abbess of Whitby, St Hilda,** is said to have performed many miraculous deeds, one of them being her triumph in **ridding the area of snakes.** She'd produce her whip, and neatly slice off the heads of the troublesome serpents.

**In later years, the many fossils found at the foot of the Whitby cliffs were** supposed to be the results of the beheadings.

At certain times of the year, and in the late morning, St Hilda is said to manifest herself in one of the windows of the abbey, and she also, tradition has it, walks the abbey grounds.

Other ghostly sightings in Whitby include a phantom coach and horses, which comes to a juddering halt outside **St Mary's parish church**, a headless spectre who stumbles around **Fitzwilliam's Steps,** a mischievous sprite or goblin called **Hob** who causes trouble in the country lanes around the community, and a giant, called **Wade**.

And then there's the sound of the abbey's bells. Tradition has it that Henry VIII had these loaded onto a ship, to be transported to London, and for them to be melted down. But the divinity intervened, and the ship sank, just off the harbour mouth. One version of the tale tells that the bells can still be heard tolling today, when a storm is due ...

The shade of that notorious burglar, n'er-do-well and murderer **Charles (Charlie) Peace** is said to haunt the steps of **Leeds Town Hall**. An odd place to choose? Not when you discover that the building (another of the creations of Hull-born **Cuthbert Brodrick**) is built solidly over the old Central Charge Office or **Bridewell**. A Bridewell is the name for a small holding cell or prison.

***Mr Peace was one of the true penny dreadful villains of the Victorian era, a housebreaker who arguably turned the crime into a fine art.***



He was a picture-frame maker by trade, but he developed a set of skills and tools for his nocturnal activities that became the talking point of his times. He was born in **Sheffield** in 1832, and was serving an apprenticeship in a local rolling mill when he was injured in an accident, and was maimed for life – no Health and Safety legislation back then, or, more to the point, compensation. He spent no less than eighteen months in Sheffield Infirmary, and when he left, he was crippled for life.

**Charlie took to playing the violin in local pubs and in small concerts to scratch a living, and by all accounts he was quite a talented musician.**

But he was supplementing his income by robbing houses at night, and he was finally caught, appeared at **Doncaster Assizes**, and was sentenced to four years' hard labour. Charlie saw the inside of prisons at Chatham in Kent, in Wakefield (from which he attempted a daring escape) and, so legend has it, in Gibraltar.

Free at last, he returned to Sheffield, married a local widow called Hannah Ward, and became a respectable member of society, even sending his children to Sunday school.

That was all on the surface. Peace paid his attentions to another woman, a **Mrs Dyson**.

At first he and the Dysons got on well, but things started to take a different turn, and Mr Dyson took out a summons against Peace after discovering that Mrs D was having a dalliance with their neighbour.

Leaving the air to cool a little, Peace and his family upped sticks and went to Hull, where they opened an eating house. After that, he went over to Manchester, and was part of a botched burglary in Whalley Range, where he and his accomplices were spotted by a pair of alert policemen.

One of them, a **Constable Cook**, was fatally shot by Charlie at point blank range. Peace made his escape, but two brothers who lived nearby, **John and William Habron**, were arrested and charged with the murder, and both stood trial. John was acquitted, but William was convicted and sentenced to hang, and the decision was later changed – he was to serve penal servitude for life. Back on this side of the Pennines, Charlie Peace discovered that the Dysons had moved to **Banner Cross**, in the north of **Sheffield**, and quickly tracked them down. In a grim confrontation, he fired two shots at Mr Dyson, one of which missed; the other hit its target. Dyson died two hours later. Peace left the scene, made his way to **Attercliffe** railway station, and took a ticket to **Beverley**. Obviously hoping to muddle any police in pursuit, he then got off the train at **Normanton**, went on to **York**, then entrained for **Cottingham**, **Beverley** and finally **Hull**. He was having a quiet meal with his missus when they heard the police arriving, and he hid. Mrs Peace was questioned, and told the officers that she hadn't seen her husband for months ... they searched the premises, and Charlie nipped over the wall at the back of the house and was on the run again.

**By now there was a reward of £100 for his capture, and the police circulated a description of him which was less than flattering. It told anyone who was interested that the man that they were after was:**

***"thin and slightly built, from fifty-five to sixty years of age. Five-feet-four or five-feet high, grey (nearly white) hair, beard and whiskers, and lacks three fingers of his left hand, walks with his legs rather wide apart, and speaks somewhat peculiarly, as if his tongue was rather too wide for his mouth. He is a great boaster."***

Hardly very flattering, but enough to mark him out in a crowd – except that

Peace was only forty-four at the time, and had only lost one finger – probably self-inflicted when he was playing around with one of his pistols.

Charles, ever resourceful, went to **Nottingham**, took lodgings in a house where the landlady specialised in dealing in stolen goods, and also took a mistress, **Susan Ward**.

**He found time to construct a false arm for himself to hide his disability.**

As soon as Peace hit Nottingham, the burglary rate went up alarmingly, and Peace was once again a wanted man.

On one occasion he gave the police the slip when he was found in bed with Susan. He pleaded for a little privacy to get dressed, and as soon as the officers granted his wish, was out and away through the window.

He returned to Hull, found his wife and family the centre of police attention, and decided that it would be easier to live somewhere else. He chose south London. Nothing if not bold, Peace rented two houses, one for his wife and child, and the other for his mistress, and the ménage moved around a bit,

**Charles maintained a business as a musical instrument dealer, and also started to work on various inventions, some of which were patented. He was no fool.**

**Unbelievably, he had a meeting with the eminent Samuel Plimsoll (he of the line on ships) at the House of Commons to discuss a device he'd dreamed up, to raise submerged vessels. He also dabbled with a smoke helmet for firemen, a form of hydraulic tank, and an improved device for washing railway carriages.**

from Lambeth to Camberwell, from Greenwich to Peckham. Meanwhile, the number of burglaries in Blackheath and district rocketed, and it was on the night of 10th October 1878, that fate and Charles Peace came face to face. He was in the middle of robbing a house in **St John's Park** when the police arrived.

Battle commenced and Peace fired five shots, four of which providentially missed their targets, but the fifth tore into the arm of a **Constable Robinson**. That didn't stop the gallant officer from holding on to Peace, and finally arresting him.

True to form, Peace gave a false name when he appeared in court the next day, where he was described as being

*"about sixty years old, and of repellent aspect."*

Charming. It was then that his loyal Susan showed her true colours, and shopped her man for a reward of £100.

**On 19th November 1878, John Ward, alias Charles Peace, was put on trial at the Old Bailey, accused of burglary and the attempted murder of PC Robinson.**

**He was sentenced to penal servitude, even though he acted the part of someone prematurely senile in the dock, and almost convinced the judge of being slow-witted.**

He was then taken by train to **Sheffield** to be indicted of the murder of Dyson, and outwitted his prison guards as the train neared **Worksop**, making his escape through an open window. He was recaptured, rather badly injured, and taken to Sheffield Police Station. A doctor later passed him as fit to stand trial, and Peace appeared on 30th January to answer charges. Anticipating wild public interest in the case, the court sat, in candlelight, in a corridor of the town hall, where Charlie was denied an audience, and complained a lot about feeling rather cold.

**He was found guilty of Dyson's murder – Mrs Dyson was brought back from America, to where she had emigrated – to give evidence. At one point Charlie told one of his warders that if he'd really meant to kill Dyson, he would have gone about it rather more efficiently.**

Found guilty, he was hanged in **Armley Gaol**, **Leeds**, on 25th February. But he did do one honourable thing. He confessed to the murder of Constable Cook in Manchester and as a result William Habron was freed, and paid a generous sum in compensation for his false imprisonment.

Peace's incredible life of crime, his defiance of the law and his escapes soon became the stuff of legend far beyond the boundaries of Yorkshire.

***Peace was fond of saying:***
***"Lion-hearted I've lived, and when my times comes, lion-hearted I'll die."***

**On the morning of his execution he had a hearty breakfast of bacon, and on the gallows asked twice for a glass of water. His final requests were refused him.**

His name made its way into two novels, one of them a Sherlock Holmes mystery, and there were other books, many poems and piles of pamphlets about him. There were two films later made about his exploits, one of which occasionally crops up on Channel 4 in the afternoon schedules.

***And then there's his ghost at Leeds Town Hall*** ... which is a bit odd, because the splendid edifice was in fact built between 1853 and 1858, long before Peace's death, and a few miles away from Armley where he met his end. You can, perhaps, put any sightings of Charlie to merely being part of the incredible lore and legend that surrounds such a flamboyant villain.

It is said that, once in a very rare while, the clock at **Leeds Town Hall** strikes an ominous chime of thirteen.

When that happens, time is frozen, the entire city (and presumably the world) stands momentarily still, and the four white lions that guard the building slowly begin to move, and then take a stroll around their territory.

**They then return to their plinths, and when that happens, everything begins to move again.**

There is, says this story, proof of this happening – when the lions go back into position, they are never quite as they were before. There are tiny differences in their facial expressions and in their posture. But you'd have to be an expert to notice.

And no account of things ghostly in the county would be complete without our dear old friend **Mary Queen of Scots**, who pops up every now and then to surprise the unwary at **Nappa Hall**, in **Askrigg**. The hall is a fifteenth-century fortified manor house, and Mary stayed there in 1568, while a prisoner of Elizabeth I. She was also held at **Bolton Castle**. There was a lurid account of the appearance of Mary's ghost written by a visitor to the hall in 1878. As **Sir Noel Coward** wrote, in the lyrics to ***The Stately Homes of England***,

*"If anyone spots the Queen of Scots, in a hand-embroidered shroud ... "*

Well, at least one guest at Nappa did.

**Gormire Lake**, surrounded by the stunning **Garbutt Wood**, was created by the effects of glaciation, and is one of the few natural stretches of water in Yorkshire.

The lake is woven into the myths of time, one of them concerning a witch who was being pursued across the nearby moors. **When she came to White Mare Crag she leapt into the air and fell into the Lake,** which, by the way, is also said to have a submerged village deep in its watery depths. The witch was picked up by an underwater current, **and finally emerged from a well nine miles away.**

There's also the yarn of a goose which was dropped into the lake, and finally popped up again in **Kirkbymoorside**, sans feathers. Even Paul Daniels would be hard-put to pull that trick off. Kirkbymoorside is twelve miles east of the lake.

**The Great North Road** near **Boroughbridge** is haunted by **Tom Hoggett**, a notorious vagabond and highwayman, who drowned in the River Swale, attempting to avoid capture. His ghost wears a very long glowing coat, and travels the road at a great speed.

Flixton is haunted by **its very own werewolf,** a legend that seems to go back all the way to Saxon times…

In a more recent age, many of Yorkshire's old airfields are said to be haunted by the restless dead of the Second World War, airmen who died on, or returning to, their bases. **Leeming** is a good example of this, and many of the long-gone lads have appeared in full RAF uniform, and some claim to have heard their voices.

Another leap from the **White Mare Crag** concerns an **abbot of Rievaulx Abbey** and a certain nobleman called **Sir Harry de Scriven**. It pops up in the form of a very long and doggerel-like ***'poem'*** in a book of folklore published by the fragrantly-named **Edmund Bogg**, published in 1894. It is all about the rivalry between the two men, and in particular their love of their fine horses, one of which, **Nightmare**, flies over the edge of the Crag and into the water beneath.

The knight is described thus:

***Sir Harry came of Old Yorkshire stock,***
***The finest chip of a rare old block,***
***The huntingest Squire***
***In the huntingest Shire***
***His nerve never failed, his limbs would not tire,***
***A rollickinging son of a rollicking sire.***

Which will give you some idea of the quality of the rest of the verse.

The abbot, like a lot of his contemporary clergymen, had his mind on things other than the scriptures and divine service, and was particularly proud of his white Arab mare. But at one point in the story:

***Then the Abbot was called to visit the sick,***
***Sir Harry was charmed, and called him a brick,***
***But inwardly smiled at the fun of his trick,***
***And, under his breath,***
***Wished him soon with Old Nick.***

It goes on in the same vein. And on …

**That eminent man of the theatre and tragedian Sir Henry Irving is said to haunt the stage and backstage area of Bradford's Theatre Royal – not the Bradford Alhambra as often erroneously stated.**

The Royal was demolished in 1989, so what happened to Sir Henry's unhappy shade after that is anyone's guess.

He had finished appearing in the play ***Becket*** at the venue on Manningham Lane, and went back to his hotel, the **Midland**, happily still standing. But Sir Henry was not standing himself for very long, for the very first actor to be knighted by his gracious sovereign (Victoria) collapsed and died in a chair in the foyer. The chair was subsequently bought from the management of the hotel by the members of the **Garrick Club**, in London, where it still remains.

Irving's ashes were buried in Westminster Abbey – the first person of note to have his ashes rather than his body interred there. He died in 1905, and the last lines of the play, and the last lines that Irving spoke were:

**"Into thine hands, O Lord!"**

Oddly, Irving's death was on Friday, 13th October. He was sixty-seven.

Irving's personal assistant, manager of his Lyceum Theatre (in London), biographer and close friend of many years was ***Dracula*** author, **Bram Stoker**, who was with him as **The Guv'nor** (as he was affectionately called) breathed his last.

Yorkshire's ghosts take a bit of beating, for sheer range of reasons of returning to this mortal coil, if nothing else.

Let's start with the weeping woman of **Rossington**, who is said to be the shade of a lady ill-treated by a Roman soldier. She sobs away in the shadows of an evening, and is half-naked. The suburb of Doncaster was once a small Roman settlement called ***Brementium*** and the much larger Doncaster was, in the times of the Roman occupation, ***Danum***.

The most famously documented Roman ghosts of Yorkshire are in York itself, **in the Treasurer's House,** which is owned by the National Trust.

There, one day in 1953, an apprentice plumber who was working in the cellar and helping to put in central heating, heard the sound of a horn. He thought nothing more about it, **and then a spectreal horse walked through the brickwork.** The lad fell off his ladder in shock.

**After the horse came a line of Roman soldiers,** all looking very tired and dejected. They were certainly not going out to battle full of joie de vivre, and appeared to be returning in very low spirits.

The apprentice then noticed that they all seemed to be missing the lower part of their legs – but then realised that of course the ground levels had risen over the centuries.

The last of the line walked into view. He was carrying a very battered long trumpet. **Could this have been the remnants of the fabled Ninth Legion,** who marched out of York one day, to harry the tribes beyond Hadrian's Wall, but who never returned?

They were made famous in **Rosemary Sutcliffe**'s bestseller ***The Eagle of the Ninth***, which was released as the film ***The Eagle*** early in 2011. Who knows? But the young man, who swore blind that what he'd seen was an honest account of the event, later stopped his apprenticeship. And became a bobby in the York police force.

Then there's another rather better-known lady than her Rossington sister, this time Emily Brontë, who strolls the paths alongside the waterfall near Haworth. In 1978, on the anniversary of her death, one of Yorkshire's most famous daughters visited Weaver's Restaurant in the town, and apparently climbed a staircase that had been removed years before. The sight must have given the shocked diners very good value for money.

Rather more malevolent is the ghost of **Gillamoor**, where poor old **Kitty Garthwaite** attempts to lure passers-by into the River Dove. Kitty was wronged by her lover, and found herself pregnant. In shame, she drowned herself, and trying to get others to follow her fate is her revenge.

At Long Marston there's a veritable gaggle of ghosts, all soldiers killed fighting in the **Battle of Marston Moor** in 1644, in which **Oliver Cromwell** was victorious in the fight against the Roundheads.

**At least three gentlemen in full cavalier costume have been spotted, recently by a couple of motorists on the A59 York to Harrogate road.**

The screams and wails of soldiers from both sides in the conflict have also been heard, and the nearby Old Hall, at which Cromwell (who at that time held the rank of lieutenant general) was billeted, is haunted by old 'General Ironsides' himself.

At **Coverham** a Black Lady walks from the church over the moor toward **Middleham**. She is said to be a woman whose body was discovered in the middle of the last century, by lads out digging for peat.

At Fountains Hall there's a Blue Lady, allegedly the shade of the daughter of Sir Stephen Proctor, who built the place. He was known to be an appallingly evil man, and the lass is claimed to have witnessed some of his dirty doings.

**And a man dressed in clothing of the Elizabethan period sometimes manifests himself through the wooden panelling of the stone hall. Nasty. And messy.**

**"Well I Never!"**

Near **Wakefield**, there used to stand a fine old building called **Heath Hall**, which was the home of one **Mary Bolles**, and she decreed in her will that the room in which she died should be permanently sealed off, wherever in the house it might be. Her will was observed when Mary went to meet her maker in 1661. For fifty years it remained shut, but in 1711 some daft soul decided that enough was enough, and re-opened it. From that moment on, Mary roamed the house, and was never stilled. There were supplications at her tomb in **Ledsham Church**, but the old gal wouldn't give up. Sadly, the hall was demolished, but the door to the room is carefully preserved in **Wakefield's Museum**.

**During the Second World War troops stationed in the house spotted her many times, and one caretaker insisted that none of his guard dogs would ever go near Mary's room.**

There are other colourful ladies present at **East Riddlesden Hall** – there's a Grey Lady who was starved to death by her husband, and who gently rocks a cradle while weeping, a Blue Lady wanders the grounds, and a White Lady haunts the pond where she tragically drowned.

The trio is kept company by a Scottish merchant who was murdered by an avaricious steward while visiting the hall.

***East Riddlesden is probably not the place you'd choose to spend a peaceful night of unbroken sleep.***

Yorkshire pubs are a great place to find spirits (dreadful pun intended); take **Old Boots**, at the **Unicorn Hotel** in **Ripon**'s lovely market square. **Tom Crudd** was his real name, and he was bootboy at the hotel until his death in 1762.

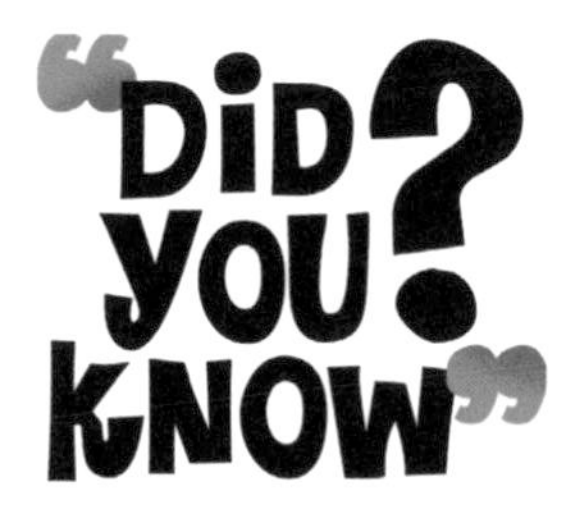


**Tom's great claim to fame was that he could hold a golden guinea coin between his nose and his chin, and frequently did so to amuse the visitors and to earn tips for demonstrating this rather bizarre trick. He must have looked a little like the popular caricature of Mr Punch.**

**The Busby Stoop** in **Sand Hutton** gets its name from a nasty incident in 1702 when **Tom Busby** bludgeoned his father-in-law to death by hitting the older man with a claw-hammer. Gruesome. Tom was tried, found guilty, and hanged from a gallows specially erected outside the pub. If you see him, there will be a noose around his neck, and he (unsurprisingly) holds his head at an odd angle.

And at **Kippax** you might well encounter the ghost of a former landlord at the **Old Tree Inn**. He is said to take the form of a hazy white light, and to pull himself the odd pint and to tamper with the bottles.

One of the proud Freemen of Doncaster is the hugely popular singer **Lesley Garrett**, who was born in **Thorne**, and who still has a home in nearby **Epworth**.

Lesley reveals that one of the ***'rights'*** that the position of Freeman endows upon the holder is that of grazing her cattle, sheep and poultry on the town's common lands. ***"Sadly, I have none of those animals – yet,"*** she says.

"But another right, I believe, is that if ever I were to be arrested and locked up, as a Freeman I am entitled to a single occupancy cell. I sincerely hope that I'm never in that position, but you never ever know when privileges like that might come in handy!"

**Arthur Wharton** (1865-1930) was the first professional black player in English football. Wharton was born in **Jamestown, Gold Coast** (now Accra, Ghana) and was the son of a half-Grenadian and half-Scottish father and a Ghanaian mother who was a member of the loyal royal family. He came to Britain in 1882 to train as a Methodist missionary, but abandoned that career path to become a full-time athlete. Wharton, who was something of an all-round sportsman, played as an amateur for several teams, before signing professional papers for **Rotherham** in 1889. In 1894 he transferred to **Sheffield United**. His later life was a sad one, and he died a penniless alcoholic.

**His grave in Edlington cemetery, near Doncaster, was unmarked until very recently, when a group called Football Unites, Racism Divides campaigned successfully for his recognition.**

**Henry Hindley** is one of the ***'forgotten sons'*** of Yorkshire, and ought to be far better remembered – and celebrated.

Born in 1701 in **York**, he died in 1771. He was a clockmaker and a maker of scientific instruments at a time when there was a thirst for knowledge about the wonders of the world and for science in general.

Hindley invented the screw-cutting lathe, and created one of the first dividing engines, which are devices essential for the construction of accurate graduated arcs on scientific instruments. **He built a clock for York Minister** (he never seems to have strayed very far from the city) in 1752, **and is also credited with building the world's first equatorially-mounted telescope,** which can be seen at Burton Constable Hall.

He was also a close friend and companion of fellow-Yorkshireman **John Smeaton** (1724-1792) who was born in **Austhorpe** in **Leeds**, and was a phenomenal civil engineer who designed and had built – among other things – the **Ripon Canal**, the **Calder and Hebble Navigation**, the third **Eddystone lighthouse**, the **Birmingham and Fazeley Canal**, and **St Austell's Charlestown Harbour**, in **Cornwall**.

Smeaton (who was educated at **Leeds Grammar School**) met Hindley through their love of, and fascination for, mathematical instruments, and he was no mean inventor in his own right.

He died after suffering a stroke in the garden of the family home in Austhorpe, and is buried at nearby Whitkirk, in the parish churchyard of **St Mary's**.

**John Smeaton Community School** in Leeds is named after him, as is a viaduct on the final stages of the Leeds inner ring road.

Smeaton must be the only canal-builder and engineer to be mentioned in a pop music song. Yes, John Smeaton's name is in the lyrics of ***I Predict a Riot***, by the Leeds indie rock band **Kaiser Chiefs**.

***Smeaton's coefficient, a lift equation, was also used by the aviation pioneers the Wright Brothers in their attempts to become airborne.***

**Queen Victoria** wore **Whitby Jet jewellery** after the death of her beloved **Prince Albert** in 1861. It is very easy to carve, but it needs a skilled touch, because the stone is very easy to break. The jet at Whitby is of the early **Jurassic** period, which dates it to be around 182 million years old. It is not considered to be a true mineral, rather a mineraloid, since it was formed from decayed wood put under extreme pressure.

The Queen's 'promotion' of jet caused the minor gemstone to gain incredible popularity with her female subjects during the rest of her reign, **and into the Edwardian era.**

"DID YOU KNOW?"

**Berwick Kaler** is Britain's longest-serving pantomime dame, and holds the record for the number of unbroken consecutive years that any person has appeared annually in one venue – ***Jack and the Beanstalk*** in 2010 was his thirty-second consecutive year at **York's Theatre Royal**. Kaler, born in 1947, writes the shows, and co-directs them, and has, over the years, built a team of stalwart veterans around him, among them Martin Barrass and David Leonard, who are all firm favourites with the audiences.

Kaler's surreal absurdities have made the Theatre Royal's panto **one of the most successful and longest running in the country,** and he has been made a **Freeman of the City of York** and has received an **Honorary Degree from York University.**

Berwick Kaler remains modest about his achievements and his scripts.

Following in the footsteps of Jean Alexander and BBC *Look North* presenter Harry Gration, the year 2010 saw Berwick turn on the Christmas lights in the village of Burn – he turned up dressed as Queen Victoria. The Burn inhabitants were so delighted with this that they made him an Honorary Dame of Burn.

***"It's the same old rubbish,"*** he says of his pantos, ***"but it is good-quality rubbish."***

If you are a driver, then you'll take them totally for granted. But imagine the problems if the humble **Catseyes** were removed from the road.

Well, back in the early 1930s, the motorist **Percy Shaw** (of **Boothtown**, in **Halifax**) was driving along on a foggy night when he realised that the highly polished and reflective tram tracks that he'd used to guide himself home had been removed. **How was he going to steer the car efficiently?**

Shaw, who had been brought up in a humble family (his father James had been a dyehouse labourer before setting up his own small machine tools business), put his inventive mind to the thorny problem, and came up with small spheres of glass, set into the road, which would beam back the illumination of a headlight.

Well, that's version number one of the invention of catseyes. Because Mr Shaw seems to have been as inventive about the origins of the simple but hugely effective catseye as he was with things in his workshop.

***Another version he gave was of his seeing reflective studs on a road sign, and wondering why they couldn't be set in the Tarmac.***

A third was of seeing a real-life cat sitting on a wall on a pitch-black night, and noting how the car lights picked out the narrowed eyes of the moggie, and yet a fourth came back to the tram lines version, but this time the lines weren't missing at all, by gleaming in the moonlight.

You pays your money, and you makes your choice.

**In any event, Shaw's nifty invention was patented in 1934, and he set up a company called Reflective Roadstuds to manufacture the device. It caught on properly when war came in 1939, and the government brought in the blackout.**

At one point, Reflective Roadstuds made more than a million of their Catseyes, which were exported all over the world, and which have doubtless saved thousands of lives.

Shaw became more and more eccentric as he grew older, and had four television sets in his home, **Boothtown Mansion**. One was tuned to BBC1, another to BBC2, and a third to ITV. A fourth was kept in reserve. How he would have coped in this multi-channel society of today is anyone's guess.

Shaw (who was born in 1890) was awarded an OBE in 1965, which many felt was a) long overdue and b) not the honour he should have received – why wasn't he knighted?

He removed much of the furniture from his home, and also the carpet, and he never married. His one luxury was his **Rolls Royce Phantom**, and the legend was that he was a multi-millionaire many times over. That was not the case, for when he died in 1976, at the ripe old age of eighty six, he was found to have left, when probate was settled, the sum of £193,500.

Which is, considering he gave us arguably one of the greatest inventions of last century, not a lot of cash. Percy Shaw kept his eye on the road, but maybe he didn't keep quite such a careful eye on his finances?

The Americans can have their evening of Trick or Treat, but research has shown that the whole industry that has grown up around Hallowe'en was, in fact, begun in Yorkshire – as **Mischief Night**.

When many Yorkshire folk emigrated to the USA during the Industrial Revolution they took their customs with them, and the whole idea morphed into what it is today. In **Sheffield** they have gone back to the roots of the event in recent years, with thousands taking part in a very public **Fright Night** throughout the city.

Traditionally, Mischief Night (or 'Miggy Night') takes place on 4th November and takes the form of outrageous conduct being perpetrated on the unsuspecting ... putting jam or other sticky substances on house doorknobs, ringing the doorbell and running away, removing the gates to gardens – all are among the many activities.

One once-eager prankster has revealed that a common assumption when he was a Yorkshire lad was that what he was doing was completely legal on Miggy Night,

***"no copper could arrest you on that particular evening."***

He described today's Trick and Treating as ***"legalised and disguised begging, all treat and never a trick,"*** while defending Miggy Night as

***"violent, shameful chaos, which is seen as every kid's right!"***

Back in 1919, just after the guns of World War II were silenced, the village priest at **Ampleforth** decided that the cemetery of the church would be enhanced by a large wooden crucifix. Asking around, he was told that the man for the job was the carpenter **Robert Thompson**, whose passion was for working in oak.

Robert was commissioned, and so impressed were the passers-by that other orders started flowing in. They were for some pretty classy customers, including **Gilling Castle** and **Ampleforth Abbey and School**.

**What set aside each piece was** that Robert put his 'trademark' on it – **a little mouse carved somewhere on the surface.** As his fame grew and grew other churches wanted his pews, pulpits, altar rails ... and lay folk put in requests for his beautifully crafted furniture, **all made at his workshops in Kilburn.**

Robert's legacy is a thriving firm of today, busy with orders, and selling to satisfied customers from all over the world. It is an international business.

## *But why the mouse?*

*This dates from a time when Robert was still a young man, and, while working in a church with a colleague, the other lad observed that the pair were **"as poor as church mice"**.*

This struck a chord, and from that day he carved his wee emblem on everything he created.

In the village of **Thwaite**, in **Swaledale**, there is another example of some fine carving, but this time in stone.

## YORKSHIRE GREATS

On the lintel of a cottage in the centre of the community you'll find a fine example of the work of the brothers **Richard and Cherry Kearton**, a depiction of birds and animals.

Richard was born in this house in 1862, and Cherry a few years later, in 1871. An accident prevented Richard from involving himself in the usual rough and tumble games that the other village lads enjoyed, and instead he developed an interest in nature and the wildlife of the Dales. He loved the birdlife in particular. In 1882 he went to London, where he found work with the publishers, **Cassells**, and went on to be an acclaimed lecturer and author. His brother Cherry shared his interests, but his artistic skills lay in the fast-growing field of photography, and his photographs were used to illustrate Richard's

**Their first book together was *British Bird's Nests, Eggs and Egg Collecting*,** which became the very first book ever to feature photographs taken direct from Mother Nature herself. It also became the book that went straight onto the 'wish list' of every small boy eager to start a hobby – in the days before collecting birds' eggs was proscribed by law.

Cherry Kearton was a pioneer in the field of natural history photography, and later moved into film, travelling internationally to find his subjects – a David Attenborough of his day. The BBC's Natural History Unit in Bristol owes him a great deal.

copious books. Members of the Kearton family are buried in **Muker churchyard**, and there are plaques to commemorate the lives of these two gentle gentlemen set into the wall of their former school.

**John Carr,** the prolific architect (1723-1807), has the distinction of being buried in a church which he designed and also paid for, at **Horbury**, near **Wakefield**. Carr's long (and hugely profitable) career was entirely due to his decision to stay in Yorkshire rather than moving to London, as he believed that he could make a more than respectable living by building in the county. He was right.

Carr, who was twice **Lord Mayor of York** (in 1770 and 1785), died at his own home, **New Lodge**, near **Barnsley**. He had, of course, designed it himself.

No job was too small for Carr, and while his work can be enjoyed in places as far apart as Buxton in Derbyshire and Oporto in Portugal, the bulk of his work was on his native turf – everything from racecourse stands to courthouses and prisons, churches a-plenty, dozens of grand houses (including Fairfax House in York and Harewood House) and two score and more bridges, most of which are still in daily use.

If you were in service in years gone by, and the Master (or Mistress) asked you to jump, then your response, as a loyal servant, would have been ***"How high?"*** But it's a pretty sure bet that **Sir George Cayley's coachman** didn't know what he was letting himself in for when he joined the staff at **Brompton Hall**, which lies betwixt Scarborough and Pickering.

Sir George (born in the December of 1773 at **Paradise House** near **St Mary's Church** in **Scarborough**) was the head of the household, and his passion was for the skies and for the infinite possibilities of flight. In fact he has been called ***'The Father of Aeronautics'***, and there is a plaque to his memory on the wall of his birthplace. He designed a number of ***'flying devices'***, and also the first moveable rudder or tailplane which enabled a pilot to manoeuvre his craft. There was also a wheeled undercarriage.

In 1853 the first man-carrying flight in a heavier-than-air machine (as opposed to a balloon ascent) took place at Brompton. Who was the aviator? Sir George's coachman, who climbed into the rudimentary aircraft and, with a shove and a following wind, managed to go right across the valley. No light alloy engine existed to power the journey. When he emerged from the experience, the loyal servant told Sir George in no uncertain terms that he had been engaged to drive the coach and horses, and nowt more. Flying was emphatically NOT part of his duties. Sir George's reply is not on record.

The pioneer died in 1857. Move over Montgolfier and the Brothers Wright, Sir George of North Yorkshire got in there first.

The man who started the world-famous Bettys was **Frederick Belmont,** a Swiss confectioner.

**Legend has it that when he arrived in Britain, Belmont had little English, and found himself at Kings Cross Station, confused as to where his destination was.**

An elderly gentleman, who knew a little French, managed to get some sense out of Belmont, and told him he should be taking the train for **Bradford**. Belmont then went up to railway company employees, asking them about the time for the next train to ***'Bradfat'***. In the 1960s Bettys joined forces with another local firm, **Taylor's of Harrogate,** makers of Yorkshire Tea among many other brands.

Bettys have always refused to open branches outside Yorkshire, believing that with a small and compact chain, they can keep an eye on quality and service.

It is not known why the business is called Bettys.

**One theory is that it is a tribute to Elizabeth Bowes-Lyon, later Duchess of York, Queen Consort and then Queen Mother – but she wouldn't have been well-enough known in 1919.**

Was it named for Betty Lupton, former manager of the Harrogate Spa?

**or for an exuberant child who was at the meeting when the name was being discussed?**

It seems likely that we shall never know for sure.

Welcome
to
BRADFAT

# YORKSHIRE GREATS

**Andrew Marvell**, one of the early Metaphysical Poets, was born in **Winestead-in-Holderness** in 1621, and moved with his family to **Kingston-upon-Hull** when his father (also called Andrew) was appointed Lecturer at Holy Trinity Church. Marvell was a colleague and friend of John Milton, and is linked with John Donne and George Herbert. He was a Parliamentarian, and died in 1678, long after Charles II had been restored to his throne.

He was only twelve when he went to **Trinity College**, **Cambridge**, and he then toured extensively in Europe, learning several languages en route. On his return he was for a while tutor to the daughter of the military strategist **Colonel Thomas (Black Tom) Fairfax**, another Yorkshireman. He became a respected and conscientious MP, and an agent for **Hull Trinity House**, representing their interests in London.

Marvell's most famous poems are *To His Coy Mistress*, *The Garden* and *Upon Appleton House*

Marvell – who was no Puritan, although he was no Royalist either – has a statue to him in the centre of Hull, and also a school named after him.

**Many of his poems were not published until three years after his death, in 1681. His canny old housekeeper Mary Palmer had hung on to them, but public opinion of her diminished when, with no evidence to support it, she claimed to have been his wife.**